WJEC GCSE HISTORY

NITIN KOPPANA

Germany in Transition
1919–1939

The USA: A Nation of Contrasts
1910–1929

Steve Waugh
John Wright
R. Paul Evans

DL Dynamic Learning

HODDER EDUCATION
AN HACHETTE UK COMPANY

This material has been endorsed by WJEC and offers high quality support for the delivery of WJEC qualifications. While this material has been through a quality assurance process, all responsibility for the content remains with the publisher.

Every effort has been made to trace all copyright holders, but if any have been inadvertently overlooked, the Publishers will be pleased to make the necessary arrangements at the first opportunity.

Although every effort has been made to ensure that website addresses are correct at time of going to press, Hodder Education cannot be held responsible for the content of any website mentioned in this book. It is sometimes possible to find a relocated web page by typing in the address of the home page for a website in the URL window of your browser.

Hachette UK's policy is to use papers that are natural, renewable and recyclable products and made from wood grown in sustainable forests. The logging and manufacturing processes are expected to conform to the environmental regulations of the country of origin.

Orders: please contact Bookpoint Ltd, 130 Milton Park, Abingdon, Oxon OX14 4SB. Telephone: +44 (0)1235 827720. Fax: +44 (0)1235 400454. Email education@bookpoint.co.uk Lines are open from 9 a.m. to 5 p.m., Monday to Saturday, with a 24-hour message answering service. You can also order through our website: www.hoddereducation.co.uk

ISBN: 978 1 5104 0320 8

© R. Paul Evans, Steve Waugh and John Wright 2017

First published in 2017 by
Hodder Education,
An Hachette UK Company
Carmelite House
50 Victoria Embankment
London EC4Y 0DZ

www.hoddereducation.co.uk

Impression number   10 9 8 7 6 5 4 3 2 1

Year   2021 2020 2019 2018 2017

All rights reserved. Apart from any use permitted under UK copyright law, no part of this publication may be reproduced or transmitted in any form or by any means, electronic or mechanical, including photocopying and recording, or held within any information storage and retrieval system, without permission in writing from the publisher or under licence from the Copyright Licensing Agency Limited. Further details of such licences (for reprographic reproduction) may be obtained from the Copyright Licensing Agency Limited, Saffron House, 6–10 Kirby Street, London EC1N 8TS.

Cover photo © The Print Collector/Alamy Stock Photo © The Bain Collection via Library of Congress

Typeset in India by Aptara Inc.

Printed in Italy

A catalogue record for this title is available from the British Library.

CONTENTS

| Introduction | 4 |

Germany in Transition 1919–39

1 The impact of the First World War	6
2 The recovery of Weimar	15
3 The Nazi rise to power and the end of the Weimar Republic	22
4 Consolidation of power	40
5 Nazi economic, social and racial policy	47
6 Terror and persuasion	66
7 Hitler's foreign policy	74
Examination guidance	90

The USA: A Nation of Contrasts 1920–29

1 Immigration	101
2 Religion and race	108
3 Crime and corruption	118
4 Economic boom	127
5 The end of prosperity	135
6 Popular entertainment	142
7 Role of women	151

Examination guidance	158
Glossary	168
Index	172
Acknowledgements	175

Introduction

About the course

During this course you must study four units, each contributing a different weighting to the GCSE qualification:

- **Unit 1** Studies in depth (Wales and the wider perspective) – weighting of 25 per cent of GCSE qualification
- **Unit 2** Studies in depth (History with a European/World focus) – weighting of 25 per cent of the GCSE qualification
- **Unit 3** Thematic study, which includes the study of a historical site – weighting of 30 per cent of the GCSE qualification
- **Unit 4** Working as an historian – non-examination assessment – weighting of 20 per cent of the GCSE qualification.

These studies will be assessed through three examination papers and a non-examination unit.

Units One and Two each consist of a one-hour examination made up of a series of compulsory questions. These will focus upon the analysis and evaluation of historical sources and interpretations, as well as testing second order historical concepts.

Unit Three consists of a one-hour-and-15-minute examination made up a series of compulsory questions. These will focus upon second order historical concepts such as continuity, change, cause, consequence, significance, similarity and difference.

Unit Four will consist of a non-examination assessment. It will involve the completion of two tasks, one focusing on source evaluation and one on the formation of different historical interpretations of history.

About the book

This book covers two options for the Unit 2 Study in depth – *Germany in Transition 1919–39*, and the *USA: A Nation of Contrasts, 1910–29*. You will only need to study **one** of these options.

How this book will help you in WJEC GCSE History

It will help you learn the content

Many students worry that they won't know enough to answer the questions in the exam. The **author text** explains the key content clearly and helps you understand each of the topics. Each chapter equips you with the right level of knowledge and detail needed to help provide detailed answers for the exam.

The book is full of **sources**. History is at its best when you can see what real people said, did, felt and watched. Sources can really help you understand the story better and remember it because they help you see what the issues meant to people at the time.

The **activities** direct you to the things you should be noticing or thinking about in the sources and text. They also help you practise the kind of analytical skills that you need to improve in history.

Each chapter includes **key terms** to help you understand what these words mean so you can understand them and use them confidently when writing about the subject. They are all defined in the Glossary on pages 168–170.

It will help you prepare for your exam

The practice questions on the book are exam-style questions that give you the opportunity to practise exam skills.

The exam guidance at the end of the unit (pages 90–99 for *Germany in Transition* and pages 158–167 for *USA: A Nation of Contrasts*) contain a model exam paper as well as step-by-step-guidance, model answers and advice on how to answer particular question types in the Studies in depth (History with a European/World focus) paper.

Germany in Transition 1919–39

1 The impact of the First World War

On 11 November 1918, the armistice was signed bringing an end to fighting in the First World War (1914–18). The setting up of the Weimar Republic did not signal peace for Germany. The five years after the war were chaotic and the Republic faced a host of challenges including an attempted communist revolution, political assassinations, *Putsches* (armed uprisings) and massive inflation. Above all, Germans had to accept what they felt was a vindictive peace settlement – the Treaty of Versailles. Many Germans said that all the problems of the post-war years were the result of the decisions that had been made by the politicians of the new Weimar Republic.

The Weimar Government and its weaknesses

By autumn 1918 German defeat in the First World War seemed imminent. In October 1918 a new German government was formed, led by Prince Max of Baden. US President Woodrow Wilson refused to discuss peace terms with Prince Max and Germany while **Kaiser** Wilhelm II was in control. At the end of October the German navy mutinied and unrest began to spread across Germany. On 9 November Kaiser Wilhelm II abdicated the German throne due to his waning support and fled to Holland. As a result, a new German **Republic** was declared and Chancellor Friedrich Ebert accepted the **armistice** that ended the First World War. Many Germans saw the ending of the war as a betrayal of the German army (*Reichswehr*). From its very beginning, therefore, many Germans, especially those in the army, despised the new Republic. In the final weeks of 1918 there were attacks on the new government. Elections for a **Constituent Assembly** were held on 19 January 1919. After the elections, it was decided that Berlin was too dangerous a place for the members of the Constituent Assembly to meet. Therefore, the decision was taken to meet in the more peaceful surroundings of the town of Weimar (hence the eventual name of the new republic). The most important result of the January elections was that no single party had a majority of seats. This meant there would have to be a **coalition government**.

The Weimar Constitution

Following the abdication of the Kaiser, a new constitution had to be drawn up; this was finalised in August 1919. This was the first time that Germany had experienced **democracy**. Figure 1.1 below shows how the Constitution was organised and Source A (see page 7) shows some of its key articles.

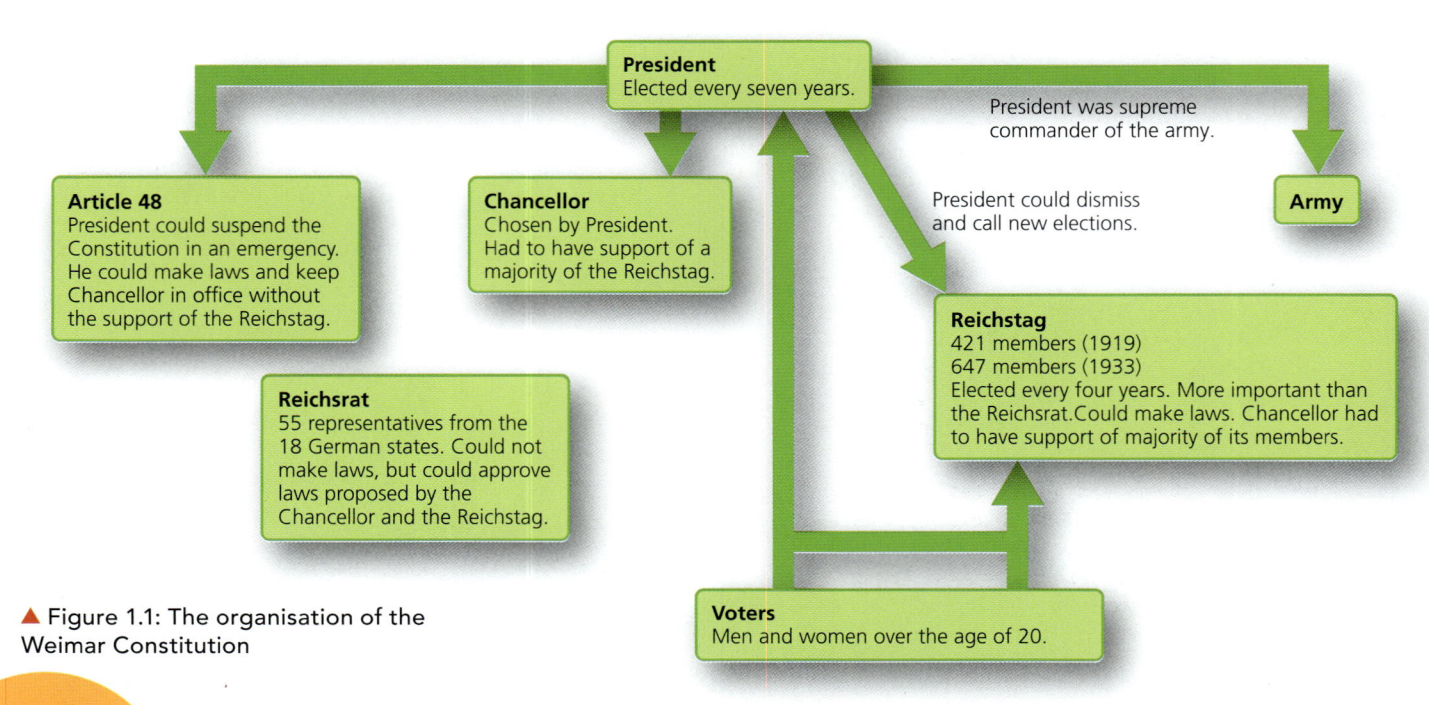

President
Elected every seven years.

President was supreme commander of the army.

President could dismiss and call new elections.

Army

Article 48
President could suspend the Constitution in an emergency. He could make laws and keep Chancellor in office without the support of the Reichstag.

Chancellor
Chosen by President. Had to have support of a majority of the Reichstag.

Reichstag
421 members (1919)
647 members (1933)
Elected every four years. More important than the Reichsrat. Could make laws. Chancellor had to have support of majority of its members.

Reichsrat
55 representatives from the 18 German states. Could not make laws, but could approve laws proposed by the Chancellor and the Reichstag.

Voters
Men and women over the age of 20.

▲ Figure 1.1: The organisation of the Weimar Constitution

1 The impact of the First World War

Source A: Key articles of the Weimar Constitution

Article 1	The German **Reich** is a republic. Political authority derives from the people.
Article 22	The Reichstag delegates are elected by universal, equal, direct and secret suffrage by all men and women over 20 years of age, in accordance with the principles of proportional representation.
Article 41	The Reich President is chosen by the whole of the German electorate.
Article 48	If public safety and order in the Reich is materially disturbed or endangered, the Reich President may take the necessary measures to restore public safety and order.

Strengths of the new Constitution

The new Constitution had several strengths:

- In some ways the laws of the Weimar Republic were very democratic. Men and women had the vote at the age of 20 at a time when in Britain the age for men was 21 and for women was 30.
- The head of the government (the Chancellor) had to have the support of most of the politicians in the Reichstag.
- A strong president was necessary to keep control over government and to protect the country in a crisis.
- Voting by **proportional representation** meant that the number of seats each party had in the Reichstag was based on the number of votes they got. For example, if a party won ten per cent of the votes it was given ten per cent of the seats.

Weaknesses of the new Constitution

Despite its strengths there were many flaws in the Constitution that contributed to the instability, weakness and eventual downfall of the Weimar Republic, particularly proportional representation and Article 48, which gave powers to the President in an emergency. Figure 1.2 summarises these weaknesses. When things did not go well for Germany in the early post-war years, politicians were criticised for creating a weak system of government (see Source B).

Source B: From a speech to the new Constituent Assembly by Hugo Preuss, head of the Commission which drew up the Weimar Constitution in 1919. He was talking about the new Constitution

I have often listened to the debates with real concern, glancing timidly to the gentlemen of the Right, fearful lest they say to me: 'Do you hope to give a parliamentary system to a nation like this, one that resists it with every sinew in its body?' One finds suspicion everywhere; Germans cannot shake off their old political timidity and their deference to the authoritarian state.

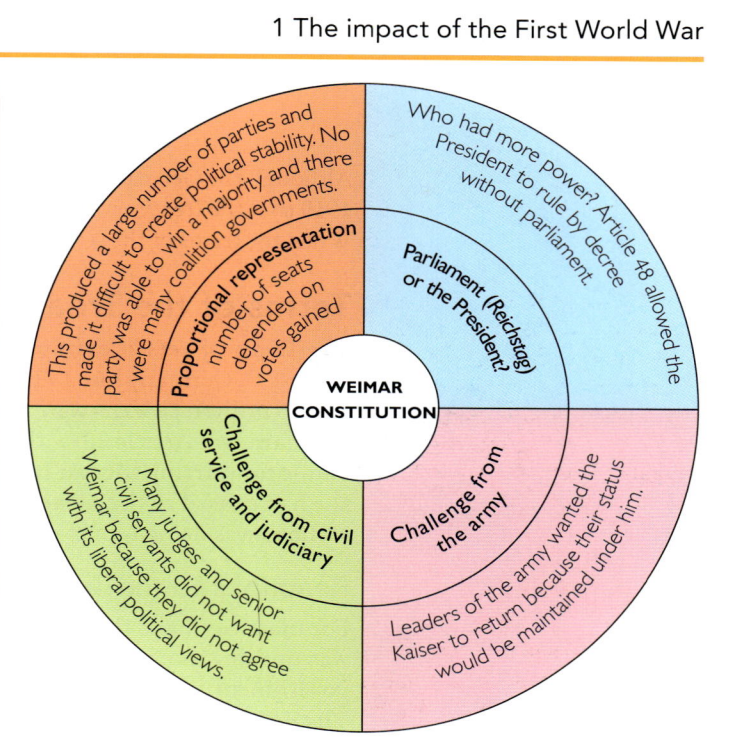

▲ Figure 1.2: Some flaws of the Weimar Constitution

ACTIVITIES

1 Study Figure 1.1 and Source A. In what ways was the Constitution democratic/undemocratic? Complete your answer using a copy of the table below.

Democratic: Government in which all the people are involved in the decisions	Undemocratic: Government in which not all the people are involved

2 Weigh up the strengths and weaknesses of the Weimar Constitution. Having read the information on this page do you agree that the Constitution made the Republic weak?

Practice question

Describe the main features of the Weimar Constitution. (For guidance, see page 93.)

The impact of the Treaty of Versailles

Although the Germans signed the armistice on 11 November 1918, it was not until 28 June 1919 that the treaty ending the First World War was signed in the Palace of Versailles in France. When the terms of the settlement were published huge numbers of Germans were horrified.

Terms of the Treaty of Versailles

The Treaty of Versailles imposed extremely severe terms on Germany (see Figure 1.3 and Table 1.1). Germany lost 13 per cent of its land, 48 per cent of its iron production and more than 6 million citizens were absorbed into other countries. Perhaps the harshest term for Germany was Article 231 – the War Guilt Clause. This stated that Germany had to accept blame for starting the war in 1914, and had to agree to pay compensation for the damage she had caused to the **Allied** powers. This was compounded when entry to the **League of Nations** was denied, thus showing that Germany was still regarded as an outcast.

Reactions to the Treaty of Versailles

For most Germans the Treaty stoked the fire of shame and humiliation. To them Versailles was nothing more than a dictated peace (*Diktat*). A scapegoat was needed – and the Weimar government and its politicians fitted the bill. Yet there was much irony in this criticism. The Weimar cabinet initially rejected the terms of the peace settlement and on 19 June 1919 Chancellor Scheidemann resigned in disgust. Leading politicians called the terms a *Gewaltfrieden* (an enforced peace). However, many believed the notion that the army had not been defeated by the Allies but had been forced to surrender by the new government. The army had been 'stabbed in the back' (**Dolchstoss**) by the politicians who signed the armistice. These politicians became known as the 'November Criminals'.

Figure 1.3: The territorial terms of the Treaty of Versailles

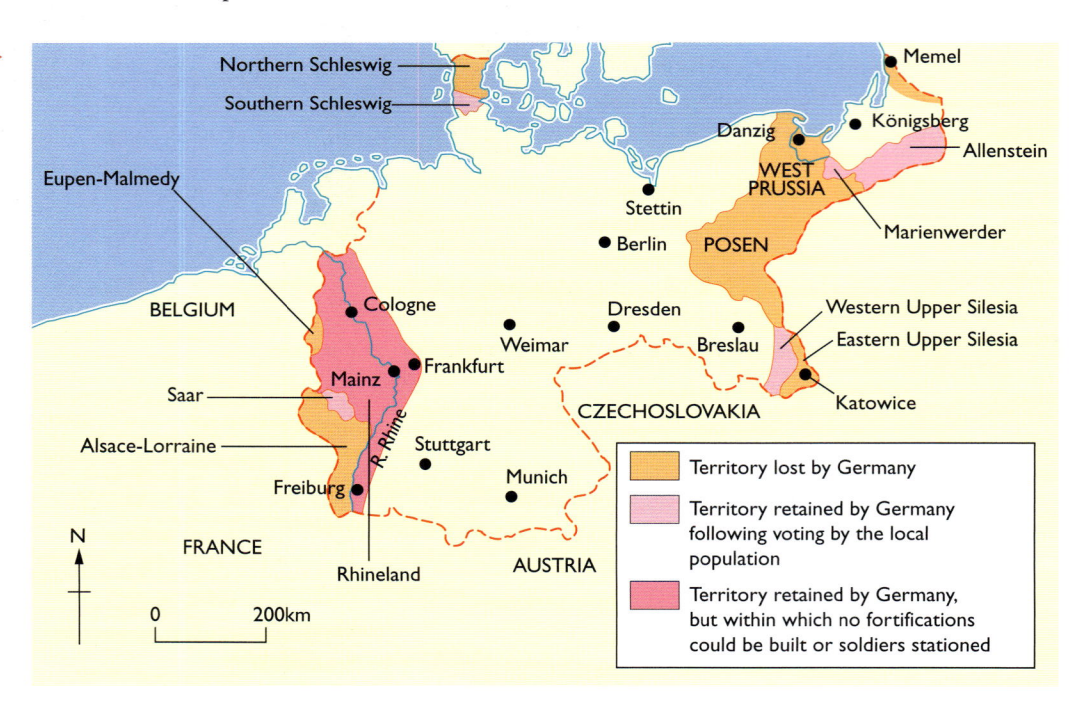

1 The impact of the First World War

Territorial terms	Military terms	Financial terms
All colonies to be given to the Allied Powers.	Army not to exceed 100,000.	Coal to be mined in the Saar by France.
Alsace-Lorraine returned to France.	No tanks, armoured cars and heavy military permitted.	Reparations fixed at £6,600 million.
Eupen-Malmedy given to Belgium after a plebiscite.	No military aircraft permitted.	Cattle and sheep to be given to Belgium and France as reparations.
Saar to be administered by the League of Nations.	No naval vessel to be greater than 10,000 tons.	Germany to build merchant ships to replace Allied ships sunk by U-boats.
Posen and West Prussia given to Poland, and Eastern Upper Silesia given to Poland after a plebiscite.	No submarines permitted.	
Danzig created a Free City.	Rhineland demilitarised.	
Memel to be administered by the League of Nations.		
No union (Anschluss) with Austria.		
Northern Schleswig given to Denmark after a plebiscite.		

▲ Table 1.1: The most important terms of the Treaty of Versailles

Source C: From a German newspaper, *Deutsche Zeitung*, 28 June 1919

Vengeance! German nation! Today in the Hall of Mirrors [Versailles] the disgraceful treaty is being signed. Do not forget it. The German people will, with unceasing work, press forward to reconquer the place among nations to which it is entitled. Then will come vengeance for the shame of 1919.

ACTIVITIES

1. Study Source C. What does it tell you about German attitudes towards the signing of the Treaty of Versailles?
2. Explain why Article 231 was hated by most Germans.
3. Work in groups of three or four. Choose territorial, military or financial terms of the Treaty of Versailles. Present a case to the class, stating why your choice has the most important consequences for Germany.
4. What do the terms 'stabbed in the back' and 'November Criminals' mean?

Practice questions

1. Describe how Germany was punished under the terms of the Treaty of Versailles. *(For guidance, see page 93.)*
2. What was the purpose of Source D? *(For guidance, see pages 94–95.)*

▲ Source D: A cartoon entitled 'Clemenceau the Vampire' from the German right-wing satirical magazine, *Kladderadatsch*, July 1919. Clemenceau was the leader of France. The cartoon is commenting on the Treaty of Versailles

Political instability

The Weimar government was initially unpopular among many Germans because it had surrendered, established a weak constitution and failed to end food shortages. Weimar was hated by communists, socialists, nationalists, army leaders and those who had run Germany before 1918. It seemed to have a bleak future. The Weimar Republic faced constant threats from the left and right and there were several uprisings across Germany that threatened the government's existence. Figure 1.4 shows the extent and duration of the unrest in post-war Germany.

After the Bolshevik Revolution in Russia in October 1917, when the Provisional (temporary) Government was removed by the communists Lenin and Trotsky, many Germans hoped that a socialist country could be established in Germany. Soldiers, sailors and workers set up councils (soviets) in October and November 1918. Because of the fear of a revolution in the chaos of the post-war period, the Weimar government made a deal with the new army leader, Groener.

It was agreed that the army would support the new government against revolution and the government would support and supply the army. Thus Weimar became dependent on the army. For some Germans this dependency on the army weakened the authority of the Weimar Republic.

> ### ACTIVITIES
> 1 Why was there a fear of a Bolshevik Revolution in Germany?
> 2 Why was the deal between Ebert and Groener significant for the Weimar Republic?

Figure 1.4: Political violence in Germany, 1919–23

1 The impact of the First World War

The Spartacist Uprising

During the war, several groups emerged from the German Social Democratic Party (SPD). The most radical was the Spartacist League led by Karl Liebknecht and Rosa Luxemburg who eventually sought to establish a state based on communist ideals. (The League took its name from the Roman slave Spartacus, who led a rebellion in 73BC.) In December 1918, the Spartacists' demonstrations against the government led to clashes with the army and resulted in the deaths of sixteen Spartacists. At the end of the month, the Spartacists formed the German **Communist Party** (**KPD** – *Kommunistische Partei Deutschlands*).

On 6 January 1919, the Spartacists began their attempt to overthrow Ebert and the Weimar government in order to create a communist state. Ebert and his defence minister, Noske, used the *Reichswehr* (regular army) and the Berlin *Freikorps* (see box) to put down the rebellion.

Within days the rising was over. The Spartacists were no match for the army and *Freikorps*. Liebknecht and Luxemburg were captured and killed. It was the violence of the rising that forced the new Assembly to move to Weimar (see page 6).

In March, a further communist-inspired rising in Berlin was put down with great ferocity and more than 1,000 people were killed. Another communist rising in Munich was crushed by the *Freikorps* with great severity in April.

> *Freikorps*
> Paramilitary groups formed from demobilised soldiers at the end of the war. They refused to give up weapons and uniforms and were led by ex-army officers. Most *Freikorps* were monarchists who sought to save Germany from Bolshevism even though they did not support the Weimar Republic. There were about two hundred different groups across Germany.

◀ **Source E:** Photograph of *Freikorps* in front of the *Vorwärts* newspaper building, which they had captured from the Spartacists in January 1919. The *Vorwärts* newspaper was a socialist newspaper

ACTIVITIES

1 Study Source E. Who were the Spartacists? Why was it important for them to control the *Vorwärts* building?
2 How did the Spartacists threaten the Weimar Republic?

Practice question

Use Source E and your own knowledge to describe the Spartacist Uprising of 1919. *(For guidance, see pages 91–92.)*

The Kapp *Putsch*

Having resisted the challenge from the left, Ebert had to face the right in 1920. When the Weimar government announced measures in March 1920 to reduce the size of the army and also disband the *Freikorps*, there was uproar in Berlin. The leader of the Berlin *Freikorps*, Ehrhardt, refused to comply. Together with a leading Berlin politician, Wolfgang Kapp, a plan was drawn up to seize Berlin and form a new **right-wing** government with Kapp as the chancellor. Kapp stressed the communist threat, the *Dolchstoss* theory (see page 8) and the severity of the Treaty of Versailles. The *Reichswehr* in Berlin, commanded by General Luttwitz, supported Ehrhardt and Kapp. Following Kapp's successful seizure of Berlin on 13 March 1920, the Weimar government moved to Dresden and then Stuttgart. The new regular army had been asked to put down the Kapp **Putsch**, but the Commander-in-Chief, von Seeckt, said 'The *Reichswehr* does not fire on *Reichswehr*.'

Ebert and Scheidemann called on the people of Berlin not to support the Kapp *Putsch* and asked them to go on strike. **Trade unionists** and civil servants supported the government and, because it had little support, the *Putsch* collapsed. More than four hundred *Reichswehr* officers had been involved in the *Putsch* but very few were punished.

Further uprisings

One week after the Kapp *Putsch* began, a communist rising occurred in the Ruhr. This time the army became involved and brutally put down the rebellion. Hundreds were killed. Violence continued in Germany during the next two years and both **left-wing** and right-wing groups were involved.

It has been estimated that there were 376 murders (354 of them were carried out by the right) in the period 1919–22. No right-wingers were sentenced to death but ten left-wingers were. Two leading Weimar ministers were assassinated during this time – in 1921, Matthias Erzberger, leader of the **Centre Party** and a signatory of the Treaty of Versailles and, in 1922, Walther Rathenau, the Foreign Minister. The final threat to Weimar in this period came in November 1923, when there was a *Putsch* in Munich, led by Adolf Hitler. This will be examined on pages 25–27.

▲ **Source F:** Soldiers and *Freikorps* troops in Berlin 1920. Note the swastika on some of the helmets and the presence of the flag of the Second Reich, the name given to the German Empire, 1871–1918

ACTIVITIES

1. What grievances did Kapp and the Berlin *Freikorps* have in 1920?
2. Which do you think posed the greatest threat to the Weimar Republic, the Spartacists or the Kapp *Putsch*? Give reasons for your answer.

Events in the Ruhr and hyperinflation

The problems facing the Weimar Republic worsened in 1923 due to the French occupation of the Ruhr and the effects of **hyperinflation**.

Germany had experienced inflation during the First World War and had borrowed extensively to finance its war effort. When the reparations figure was announced – £6,600 million at £100 million per year – the Weimar government claimed that it could not pay. Moreover, the loss of wealth-creating industrial areas exacerbated the problem. As inflation continued, the Weimar government began to print more money in order to pay France and Belgium as well as its own workers. The value of the German currency started to fall rapidly and, in 1921, because no reparations were paid, France sent troops into the Ruhr, Germany's main industrial area. The Ruhr is sited in the Rhineland so there were no German troops to stop the invading troops (see Figure 1.3 on page 8.)

The French occupation of the Ruhr, 1923

A further occupation by French and Belgium troops took place in January 1923 when Germany again failed to pay reparations to both these countries. The French were angry because they needed the money to help to pay off their war debts to the USA. The French and Belgians had decided to take the goods they needed, rather than wait for the Germans to send them.

German resistance

This time the French occupation was met with **passive resistance**. However, the resistance turned sour and Germans carried out acts of industrial sabotage. The German workers in the Ruhr went on strike as a protest against the invasion. Some strikers took more direct action and set factories on fire and sabotaged pumps in some mines so they flooded and could not be worked. A number of strikers were shot by French troops: their funerals led to demonstrations against the invasion. The occupation only served to stir up old **enmities** and remind people of the war.

The results of the occupation

The invasion certainly united the German people in their hatred of the French and Belgians. The strikers became heroes of the German people as they were standing up to the humiliating Treaty of Versailles and showing that German people had not been crushed. The German government backed the strikers and printed more money to pay them a wage. The strike meant that even fewer goods were being produced in Germany. The extra strike money plus the collapse in production turned inflation into hyperinflation (see Table 1.2).

July 1914	£1 = 20 marks
Jan 1919	£1 = 35 marks
Jan 1920	£1 = 256 marks
Jan 1921	£1 = 256 marks
Jan 1922	£1 = 764 marks
Jan 1923	£1 = 71,888 marks
July 1923	£1 = 1,413,648 marks
Sept 1923	£1 = 3,954,408,000 marks
Oct 1923	£1 = 1,010,408,000,000 marks
Nov 1923	£1 = 1,680,800,000,000,000 marks

▲ Table 1.2: The decreasing value of the mark against the pound, 1914–23

> **Practice question**
>
> Describe the French occupation of the Ruhr in 1923. *(For guidance, see page 93.)*

Hyperinflation

People with savings or on a fixed income found themselves penniless. People were quick to blame the Weimar politicians. This was yet another humiliation for the new government.

Inflation did, however, benefit certain people.

- Businessmen who had borrowed money from the banks were able to pay off these debts.
- Serious food shortages led to a rise in prices of necessities, more especially food, which helped farmers.
- Foreigners who were in Germany suddenly found that they had a huge advantage. People who had dollars or pounds found that they could change them for millions of marks and afford things that ordinary Germans could not.

In the summer of 1923, Gustav Stresemann became Chancellor and he began to steady things and introduced a new currency. The following year the new currency and loans from the USA (see page 16) enabled an economic recovery. It seemed as if the Weimar Republic had weathered the storms and could look forward to a period of stability and prosperity.

ACTIVITIES

1. Study Table 1.2 on page 13. What can you learn about inflation in Germany in the years 1914–23?
2. Why do you think people who had savings in banks suffered more than most in the period of hyperinflation?
3. Study Source H. In what ways does this source help us to understand the problems of Germany in 1923?

Practice questions

1. What was the purpose of Source G? *(For guidance, see pages 94–95.)*
2. Was hyperinflation the most serious problem facing the Weimar Republic during the early 1920s? *Use your own knowledge and understanding of the issue to support your answer. (For guidance, see pages 98–99.)*

▲ **Source G:** A cartoon published in Germany by the left-wing magazine *Simplicissimus* in 1923. Translated, the top caption reads 'Paper money' and the bottom one reads 'Bread'

▲ **Source H:** A German woman in 1923 burning currency notes, which burn longer than the amount of firewood they can buy

2 The recovery of Weimar

Following the crises of 1923, including the French occupation of the Ruhr and hyperinflation, Germany seemed to experience a period of recovery at home and abroad under the direction of Gustav Stresemann and with the assistance of American loans. This, in turn, seemed to encourage greater support for the Weimar Republic and less support for extremist parties such as the Nazis and communists. In addition to economic recovery and political stability, the period between 1924 and 1929 is often described as a golden age due to significant changes in culture, the standard of living and the position of women. However, there are different views about the extent of this recovery and not all sections of society welcomed the social developments in this period.

Recovery from hyperinflation

German economic recovery was largely due to the work of Gustav Stresemann who was able to work successfully with Britain, France and the USA to improve Germany's economic and international position.

The Dawes Plan

Stresemann realised that Germany could not afford the reparations payments and persuaded the French, British and Americans to change the payment terms through the **Dawes Plan**, which was agreed in August 1924. It was named after the US vice-president Charles Dawes, who played a leading role in setting up the plan. The main points of the plan were:

- Reparations payments would begin at 1 billion marks for the first year and would increase over a period of four years to 2.5 billion marks per year. These payments were far more sensible and manageable and were based upon Germany's capacity to pay.
- The Ruhr area was to be evacuated by **Allied** occupation troops. This was carried out in 1925.
- The German **Reichsbank** would be reorganised under Allied supervision.
- The USA would give loans to Germany to help its economic recovery.

The plan was accepted by Germany and the Allies, and came into effect in September 1924.

GUSTAV STRESEMANN 1878–1929

1878	Born in Berlin
1906	Became a Reichstag deputy
1917	Appointed leader of the National Liberal Party (renamed the People's Party in 1919)
1923	Appointed foreign secretary, a post he held until his death in 1929. From August to November, served as chancellor of Germany and persuaded workers in the Ruhr to call off their **passive resistance** to the French
1926	Awarded the Nobel Peace Prize for work he had done to improve relations between Germany and France in the 1920s
1929	Died in October, just a few weeks before the Wall Street Crash and the beginning of the **Great Depression**.

US loans

The Dawes Plan also aimed to boost the German economy through US loans, beginning with a loan of 800 million marks. Over the next six years, US companies and banks gave loans of nearly $3,000 million. US investment not only helped economic recovery, but also enabled Germany to meet the reparations payments.

The Rentenmark

The hyperinflation of 1923 had destroyed the value of the German mark. In November 1923, in order to restore confidence in the German currency, Stresemann introduced a temporary currency called the Rentenmark. This was issued in limited amounts and was based on property values rather than gold reserves. Gradually it restored the confidence of the German people in the currency. In the following year, the Rentenmark was converted into the Reichsmark, a new currency now backed by gold reserves.

The Young Plan

Although Germany was able to meet the reparations payment schedule introduced by the Dawes Plan, the German government regularly complained about the level of payments. In 1929 the Allied Reparations Committee asked an American banker, Owen Young, to investigate and he came up with a new plan for payments. The reparations figure was reduced from £6,600 million to £1,850 million. The length of time Germany had to pay was extended to 59 years with payments at an average of 2.05 billion marks per year.

The Young Plan was a considerable achievement for Stresemann, but it was severely criticised by **right-wing** politicians such as Alfred Hugenberg and Adolf Hitler who objected to any further payment of reparations, especially as these were now extended to 1988.

Extent of recovery

Compared to the years of inflation and hyperinflation there was recovery, although there are different views about the extent of this recovery.

With money flowing in from America, the economy seemed to prosper. Public works provided new stadiums, apartment blocks and opera houses. Big business had benefited from hyperinflation and had been able to pay off many of its debts and benefited from a period of industrial growth (see Figure 2.1). Many workers were generally better off during this period as wages increased and the average working day remained at eight hours. Moreover, there seemed to be better relations between workers and their employers, and industry improved with fewer strikes between 1924 and 1929. This was the result of state **arbitration** which, after 1924, took a fairly middle line in disputes, often taking the side of workers.

In addition, unemployment, which had risen to 9 million by 1926, fell to the 6 million mark over the following two years (see Figure 2.2.)

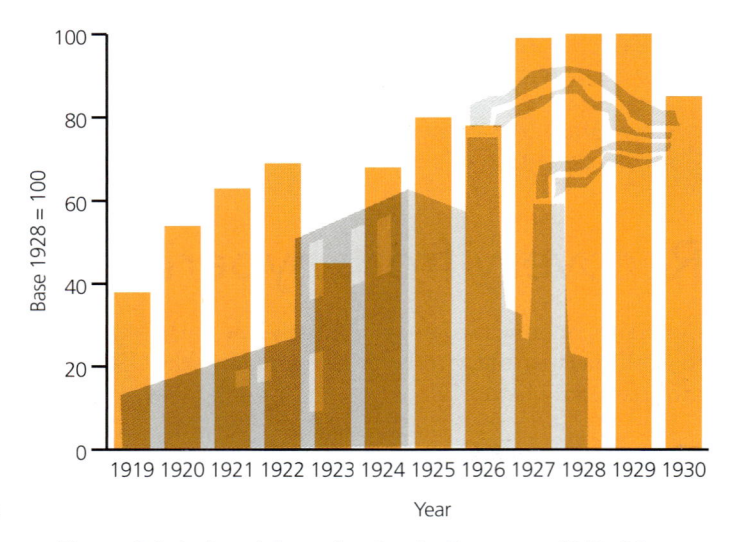

▲ Figure 2.1: Industrial production in Germany, 1919–30

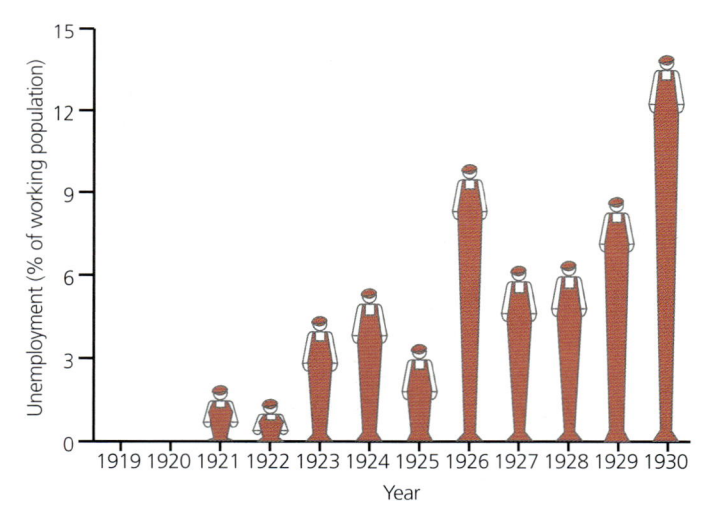

▲ Figure 2.2: Unemployment in Germany, 1919–30

2 The recovery of Weimar

Although the Weimar Republic, in the years 1924–29, seemed to recover from the problems of its first five years, the extent of that recovery has been questioned, especially the over-dependence on loans from the USA (see Source B) and the complicated situation involving loan repayments. Figure 2.3 shows that the money being borrowed from the USA was in fact being used by Germany to pay reparations to Britain and France. Britain and France then used these payments to repay loans they had received from the USA during the First World War.

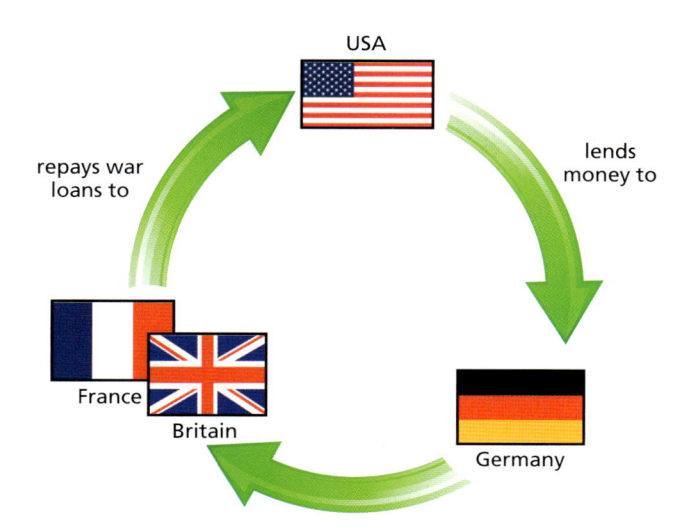

▲ Figure 2.3: The vicious circle of payments

In addition, sections of the German economy were experiencing problems, especially farmers, who experienced problems throughout the 1920s and particularly after 1927. They were affected by a worldwide depression in agriculture and needed to modernise in order to remain competitive on both the home and foreign markets. However, lack of profit led them into further debt and discouraged investment in new machinery. In 1929, when industrial production had returned to pre-war levels, agricultural production was still 74 per cent of its pre-war level.

During this period the situation improved slightly for industrial workers, whose wages increased; however, they were disappointed that the rise this was not much above the rising cost of living.

In addition, the economic recovery did not affect everyone equally. The lower middle class, whose occupations ranged from skilled craftsmen to newer jobs in the civil service, commerce and small businesses, did not fully recover from the hyperinflation of 1923. They felt that their interests were being ignored by the Weimar Republic, which seemed to favour big business.

Source A: From a German journalist, written in 1930

In comparison with what we expected after Versailles, Germany has raised herself up to shoulder the terrific burden of this peace in a way we would never have thought possible. So that today after ten years we may say with certainty 'Even so, it might have been worse'. The stage of convalescence from Versailles is a very long road to go and we have travelled it surprisingly quickly.

Source B: From a speech by Stresemann, 1929

The economic position is only flourishing on the surface. Germany is in fact dancing on a volcano. If the short-term loans are called in by America, a large section of our economy would collapse.

Interpretation 1: From *A History of Germany 1918–45*, written in 1997

However, the German recovery still had serious weaknesses. It depended on American loans which could be withdrawn at any time. Unemployment was a serious problem. The economy might be growing, but it wasn't creating jobs fast enough for Germany's rising population. Some sectors of the economy were in trouble, throughout the 1920s, farming in particular.

ACTIVITIES

1. Make a copy of the following table. Organise the information in Sources A, B and Interpretation 1 and Figures 2.1 and 2.2 into evidence for and against economic recovery. One has been done for you.

Evidence for economic recovery	Evidence against economic recovery
	Interpretation 1 suggests that Germany was too dependent on the USA

2. Using the table you made in the previous activity, write a 50-word answer to the question 'To what extent was 1924–29 a period of recovery for the Weimar Republic?'

Practice question

Study Sources A and B. Which of the sources is more useful to an historian studying the economic condition of Germany in 1930? *(For guidance, see pages 96–97.)*

Successes abroad

The Stresemann years have also been referred to as a golden age because of Stresemann's successes abroad. Stresemann, who was foreign secretary from 1923 to 1929, had several achievements abroad, including the Locarno Pact and successful relations with the League of Nations.

The Locarno Pact

Stresemann was determined to improve relations with France and Britain, partly in order to restore Germany's international prestige, but also to gain their co-operation in reducing the worst features of the Treaty of Versailles, especially reparations.

Stresemann realised that France needed to feel secure in order to co-operate over changes to the Versailles Peace Treaty. Therefore, in 1925 Germany signed the Locarno Pact with Britain, France, Belgium and Italy. By this agreement, the countries agreed to keep existing borders between Germany, Belgium and France. The Locarno Pact marked Germany's return to the European international scene and began a period of co-operation between Germany, France and Britain, sometimes described as the 'Locarno Honeymoon'.

▲ **Source C:** Stresemann signing the Locarno Pact, 1925

The League of Nations

In order for the Locarno Pact to come into operation, Germany would have to become a member of the League of Nations, an international organisation established in 1920 to try to maintain peace. In September 1926, Germany was given a permanent seat on the Council of the League of Nations. This confirmed Germany's return to Great Power status and brought considerable prestige for Stresemann. It was a bold move on his part because many Germans regarded the League as the guardian of the hated Treaty of Versailles. Moreover, Stresemann used Germany's position in the League to bring about the Young Plan (see page 16).

The Kellogg–Briand Pact

In 1928 Germany signed the Kellogg-Briand Pact along with 64 other nations. It was agreed that they would keep their armies for self-defence and solve all international disputes 'by peaceful means'.

The Pact showed further improved relations between the USA and the leading European nations, and fully confirmed that Germany was once again one of these leading nations.

The role of Stresemann

As a result of Stresemann's foreign policies:
- in 1925 France withdrew from the Ruhr
- the Allies agreed to the Dawes Plan and the Young Plan (see pages 15–16)
- in 1927 Allied troops withdrew from the west bank of the Rhine, five years before the original schedule of 1933.

Overall, Stresemann had played a crucial role in the recovery of the Republic, particularly through the Dawes Plan and American loans as well his successes abroad, which re-established the international position of Germany and brought closer relations with Britain and France. These successes made him the most popular leader of the Weimar Republic.

ACTIVITY

Source C is a photograph of Stresemann signing the Locarno Pact. Imagine you are the editor of a German newspaper in 1925 who supports Stresemann's policies. Devise a suitable caption for this photograph.

Practice questions

1. Use Source C and your own knowledge to describe the Locarno Pact of 1925. *(For guidance, see pages 91–92.)*
2. Describe how Stresemann improved Germany's relations with foreign powers between 1923 and 1929. *(For guidance, see page 93.)*

3 The Nazi rise to power and the end of the Weimar Republic

Success in the elections

When Chancellor Brüning called a general election in 1930, he was hoping to secure a clear majority for his Centre Party. However, the impact of the Wall Street Crash and the developing depression disrupted the political situation. Unemployment had hit all classes and so Hitler and the Nazis tried to appeal to all sections of society. The Nazi message was that the Weimar government had caused the economic crisis and the weak **coalition governments** had no real solutions to offer. The Nazis alone could unite Germany in a time of economic crisis.

The Nazis then played on the resentment of the Treaty of Versailles (see Source M). The old wounds were reopened and Germany's problems were blamed on the November Criminals and the Weimar Republic. Only the Nazis could restore Germany to its former glory.

> **Source M:** Part of a speech made by Hitler in Munich, August 1923
>
> *The day must come when a German government will summon up the courage to say to the foreign powers:*
>
> *'The Treaty of Versailles is founded on a monstrous lie. We refuse to carry out its terms any longer. Do what you will! If you want war, go and get it! Then we shall see if you can turn 70 million Germans into slaves!' Either Germany sinks... or else we dare to enter on the fight against death and the devil.*

If there were any who doubted the simple Nazi messages, then Hitler ensured that another scapegoat could be offered. He blamed the Jews for Germany's problems saying they:

- were involved not only with communism but also the evils of capitalism
- had helped to cause unemployment
- had conspired in Germany's defeat in the First World War
- had been involved in the Bolshevik Revolution
- were preparing to cause a revolution in Germany, which would mean that all private property and wealth would be seized by the state.

The 1930 election proved to be the breakthrough for Hitler and the Nazi Party (see Table 3.3). For Brüning, the election meant that he still had to rely on other parties and, moreover, he continued to rely on Hindenburg and Article 48 (see page 7).

Political party	Political position	September 1930	May 1928
Social Democratic Party (SPD)	Moderate	143	153
National Party (DNVP)	Right-wing	41	73
Nazi Party (NSDAP)	Right-wing	107	12
Centre Party (ZP)	Moderate	68	62
Communist Party (KPD)	Left-wing	77	54
People's Party (DVP)	Right-wing	30	45
Democratic Party (DDP)	Left-wing	20	25

▲ Table 3.3: Number of Reichstag seats after the elections of May 1928 and September 1930

ACTIVITY

Study Table 3.3. Explain why the Nazi Party had increased its support by September 1930.

The presidential election 1932

During the presidential election of 1932, when Hitler stood against Hindenburg, the Nazis were quick to use modern technology. For example, by using the aeroplane Hitler was able to speak at as many as five cities on the same day, flying from one venue to the next. Goebbels ensured that there were mass rallies, and that not only was the Nazi message being spread but also that Hitler was being recognised as a national political figure. The message was spread by films, radio and even records. Goebbels mastered the art of propaganda in these years. President Hindenburg did not campaign.

Hindenburg just failed to win more than 50 per cent of the votes in the election and so there had to be a second round of voting. Hitler was fairly successful in winning a large number of votes in each round (see Figure 3.7), though he himself was quite disappointed at his showing. Goebbels presented the presidential defeat as a victory because of the huge vote for Hitler and the overall percentage of votes won.

The tactics used by Hitler and Goebbels were paying off and there was greater success in the Reichstag elections in July 1932 (see page 38). Goebbels ensured that the German people were given positive images of Hitler and the Nazis. He also continued to play on their fears, particularly their fear of communism.

Candidate	First round	Second round
Hindenburg	18,650,000	19,360,000
Hitler (NSDAP)	11,340,000	13,420,000
Thälmann (KPD)	4,968,000	3,710,000

▲ Figure 3.7: Results of the presidential election

◀ Source N: The cover photograph of the book *Hitler über Deutschland* (*Hitler over Germany*), published in Germany in 1932

Practice question

What was the purpose of Source N? (*For guidance, see pages 94–95.*)

ACTIVITY

Read pages 28–35, copy the table below and complete the right column, giving at least one reason for each category to show how the Nazis could appeal to different groups of society at the same time.

	Appeal of the Nazis
Working classes	
Industrialists	
Middle classes	
Upper classes	

3 The Nazi rise to power and the end of the Weimar Republic

Financial support for the Nazis

Hitler and the Nazis could not have conducted their campaigns without financial backers. One example of how funds were crucial came in 1932, when 600,000 copies of the economic programme were produced and distributed in the July Reichstag election. The Nazi Party received funds from leading **industrialists** such as Thyssen, Krupp and Bosch. These industrialists were terrified of the communist threat and were also concerned at the growth of **trade union** power. They knew that Hitler hated communism and that he would reduce the influence of the unions.

Furthermore, by 1932 the Nazis had begun to develop close links with the National Party (DNVP). The DNVP leader, Alfred Hugenberg, was a newspaper tycoon and permitted the Nazis to publish articles which attacked Chancellor Brüning. Hence, Goebbels was able to continue the nationwide campaign against Weimar and keep the Nazis in the forefront of people's minds.

The communists, the second largest party, continued to offer the most serious threat to the growth of the Nazi Party (see Source O).

The SA and the communists

In his speeches, Hitler claimed that parliamentary democracy did not work and said that only he and the NSDAP could provide the strong government that Germany needed. The Nazis used their private army, *Sturmabteilung* (SA), not only to provide protection for their meetings but also to disrupt the meetings of their opponents, especially the communists. Hitler reappointed Ernst Röhm as leader of the SA in January 1931 and within a year its membership had increased by 100,000 to 170,000. These men were the 'bully boy thugs' of the Party, who loved to engage in street fights with the political opposition.

The communists had their own private army (*Die Rotfrontkämpfer* – Red Front Fighters) and there were countless fights between them and the SA (see Source P). On many occasions, there were fatalities. Hitler sought to show the German people that he could stamp out the communist violence and their threat of revolution. The SA also attacked and intimidated any overt opponents of the Nazis.

▲ **Source O:** An anti-Hitler poster by the communist, John Heartfield. Born Helmut Herzfeld, he changed his name as a protest against the Nazis. He fled Germany in 1933. Translated, the caption reads 'The meaning of the Hitler salute. Motto: millions stand behind me! Little man asks for big gifts'

▲ **Source P:** A battle between SA members and communist Red Front Fighters in 1932. Translated, the signs read 'Up the Revolution' and 'Free the political prisoners'

ACTIVITIES

1. Explain why the Nazi Party increased its financial support before the 1932 election.
2. How important were the SA in Hitler's rise to power?
3. Working in pairs, devise two captions for Source P:
   - ☐ one devised by the Nazis
   - ☐ the other devised by the communists.

35

Hitler's electoral appeal

Hitler had developed the art of public speaking in the early days of the NSDAP (see Source Q). His speeches always attracted many people and helped increase the membership of the Nazi Party. He helped to draw up the 25 Point Programme (see page 23) and he was fully aware that after the *Putsch* he had to present himself and his party as law abiding and democratic. He also knew that he had to be able to offer something to all groups in German society if he was to be successful in any elections. He never lost sight of these points during the two years before he became leader of Germany.

Hitler could be all things to all people. He was the war hero, the saviour and the ordinary man in the street. The image created was that his whole existence was given over to Germany and there were no distractions to prevent him achieving his goals. He had created a philosophy that all could comprehend. Furthermore, his vision of the future revolved around making Germany the strongest nation in the world. Hitler had the one characteristic which most other politicians lacked – charisma (see Interpretation 3 and Source S).

> **Source Q:** Part of a speech made by Hitler in Munich, August 1923
>
> *The day must come when a German government will summon up the courage to say to the foreign powers: 'The Treaty of Versailles is founded on a monstrous lie. We refuse to carry out its terms any longer. Do what you will! If you want war, go and get it! Then we shall see if you can turn 70 million Germans into slaves!' Either Germany sinks ... or else we dare to enter on the fight against death and the devil ...*

▼ **Source R:** A colourised photo of Hitler attending the Third Annual Nazi Party rally in Nuremberg, 1927

3 The Nazi rise to power and the end of the Weimar Republic

Interpretation 3: From *Inside the Third Reich* by Albert Speer, written in 1970. Speer was recalling a meeting in Berlin in 1930 at which Hitler spoke. Speer was a university lecturer and later became Minister of Armaments in Nazi Germany

I was carried away on a wave of enthusiasm (by the speech) … the speech swept away any scepticism, any reservations. Opponents were given no chance to speak … Here, it seemed to me, was hope. Here were new ideals, a new understanding, new tasks. The peril of communism, which seemed inevitably on its way, could be stopped, Hitler persuaded us, and instead of hopeless unemployment, Germany could move to economic recovery.

Source S: Adapted from the diary of Luise Solmitz, 23 March 1932. A schoolteacher, Solmitz was writing about attending a meeting in Hamburg at which Hitler spoke

There stood Hitler in a simple black coat, looking over the crowd of 120,000 people of all classes and ages … a forest of swastika flags unfurled, the joy of this moment showed itself in a roaring salute … The crowd looked up to Hitler with touching faith, as their helper, their saviour, their deliverer from unbearable distress … He is the rescuer of the scholar, the farmer, the worker and the unemployed.

ACTIVITIES

1. Study Sources Q, R, S and Interpretation 3. Make a copy of the table below and complete it to show what you can learn about the role and appeal of Hitler.

Source/Interpretation	Role and appeal of Hitler
Q	Source Q suggests that Hitler's appeal was due to his criticism of the German government …
R	
3	
S	

2. Construct a mind map to show why the Nazis had become so popular by July 1932. Begin with the most important reason at 12 o'clock and work clockwise to the least important.

Practice question

Study Sources Q and R. Which of the sources is more useful to an historian studying the reasons why many Germans voted for Hitler? *(For guidance, see pages 96–97.)*

Source T: A portrait of Hitler painted in 1933 by B. von Jacobs

Political scheming 1932–33

Hitler had been quite successful in the presidential elections in March and April 1932. He was now the leader of the second largest party in the Reichstag and was well known across Germany.

Election, July 1932

When a general election was called for on 31 July 1932, the Nazis were optimistic about improving the number of votes they had won in the previous election of September 1930.

There was much violence in the run-up to the election. About 100 people were killed and more than 1,125 wounded in clashes between the political parties. On 17 July there were at least nineteen people killed in Hamburg.

More people voted in July than in any previous Weimar election. The Nazis won 230 seats and were now the largest party in the Reichstag (see Table 3.4). However, Chancellor von Papen of the Centre Party, despite not having won the most seats, did not relinquish his post and began to scheme with President Hindenburg. Hitler demanded the post of chancellor. However, at a meeting with Hitler in August, Hindenburg refused to contemplate this, despite Hitler's leadership of the largest party in the Reichstag (see Interpretation 4).

Political party	Number of Reichstag seats	Percentage of vote
Nazis (NSDAP)	230	37.4
Social Democrats (SPD)	133	21.6
Communist Party (KPD)	89	14.3
Centre Party (ZP)	75	12.5
National Party (DNVP)	37	5.9
People's Party (DVP)	7	1.2
Democratic Party (DDP)	4	1.0

▲ Table 3.4: Results of the July 1932 general election

> **Interpretation 4:** From the book *Hitler, 1889–1936: Hubris* by Professor I. Kershaw, a specialist historian writing in 1998
>
> At the meeting in August, Hindenburg refused Hitler the chancellorship. He could not answer, he said, before God, his conscience and the Fatherland if he handed over the entire power of the government to a single party and one which was so intolerant towards those with different views.

Von Papen and the November 1932 elections

It was not possible for any party to command a majority in the Reichstag and it was impossible to maintain a coalition. Von Papen dissolved the Reichstag in September 1932 and new elections were set for early November the same year. Von Papen held the opinion that the Nazis were losing momentum and if he held on they would slowly disappear from the scene. He was correct about them losing momentum, as the results of the November general election showed (see Table 3.5).

Political party	Number of Reichstag seats	Percentage of vote
Nazis (NSDAP)	196	33.1
Social Democrats (SPD)	121	20.4
Communist Party (KPD)	100	16.9
Centre Party (ZP)	70	11.9
National Party (DNVP)	52	8.8
People's Party (DVP)	11	1.9
Democratic Party (DDP)	2	1.0

▲ Table 3.5: November 1932 Reichstag election results

Von Schleicher

However, von Papen still could not secure a majority in the Reichstag. At the same time, Hitler continued to demand the post of chancellor on the grounds that the Nazi Party was the biggest in the Reichstag. When von Papen suggested abolishing the Weimar Constitution, Kurt von Schleicher, the Minister of Defence, persuaded Hindenburg that if this happened there might be civil war.

Von Papen lost Hindenburg's confidence and resigned. He was succeeded by von Schleicher. Von Schleicher hoped to attain a majority in the Reichstag by forming a so-called *Querfront*, meaning 'cross-front', whereby he would bring together different strands from left and right parties.

Hitler becomes chancellor

Von Papen was determined to regain power and so he met with Hitler in early January 1933. It was decided that Hitler should lead a Nazi-Nationalist government with von Papen as the vice-chancellor. Scheming and plotting now took the place of considered open political debate. The army, major landowners and leaders of industry were convinced that von Papen and Hitler were saving Germany from Schleicher's plans and a possible communist takeover. The idea that von Schleicher's government might include some socialists was appalling to them.

3 The Nazi rise to power and the end of the Weimar Republic

PAUL VON HINDENBURG 1846–1934

1846	Born in Posen
1866	Joined the Prussian army
1870–71	Fought in the Franco–Prussian War
1903	Reached the rank of General
1914	Commanded German armies in East Prussia. Victorious at the Battles of Tannenberg and Masurian Lakes
1916	Made chief of general staff
1918	Retired from the army
1919	Put forward the *Dolchstoss* theory (see page 8)
1925–34	President of the Weimar Republic

FRANZ VON PAPEN 1879–1969

Career to 1933:

1879	Born in Werl, Westphalia
1913	Entered the diplomatic service as a military attaché to the German ambassador in Washington DC
1917	German army adviser to Turkey and also served as a major in the Turkish army in Palestine
1918	Left the German army. Entered politics and joined the Catholic Centre Party
1922	Elected to the Reichstag
1932	Appointed chancellor in June. Schemed with Hindenburg, thinking Hitler and the Nazis could be manipulated
1933	Appointed vice-chancellor under Hitler. Assumed Hitler could be dominated

Von Papen was able to convince President Hindenburg that a coalition government with Hitler as chancellor would save Germany and bring stability to the country. Von Papen said that he would be able to control Hitler – 'he would make Hitler squeak'.

On 30 January 1933, Adolf Hitler became chancellor of Germany. He was the leader of the largest party and he had been invited to be leader by the president. He had achieved his aim of becoming chancellor by legal and democratic means.

ACTIVITIES

1. Compare the results of the July and November 1932 elections (Tables 3.4 and 3.5 on page 38). Explain how and why they differ.
2. What is the message of the cartoon (Source U)?
3. Reread pages 38–39. The events of 1932 are complex. To simplify things, complete the table below. In each box write the main actions of each individual from mid-1932 to 1933.

Hitler	von Papen	von Schleicher	Hindenburg

4. Working in pairs, create a flow chart summarising the key political developments of 1932–33 that brought Hitler to power in January 1933.

Practice question

Was the success of the Nazis Party between 1928 and 1932 mainly due to the economic and political problems which faced the Weimar Republic at this time? *Use your own knowledge and understanding of the issue to support your answer.* (For guidance, see pages 98–99.)

▼ Source U : Cartoon from the British magazine *Punch*, January 1933, which shows Hitler being carried on the shoulders of Hindenburg and von Papen

THE TEMPORARY TRIANGLE.

Von Hindenburg and Von Papen (*together*)—
"FOR HE'S A JOLLY GOOD FELLOW,
FOR HE'S A JOLLY GOOD FELLOW,
FOR HE'S A JOLLY GOOD FE-EL-LOW,
(*Aside:* "Confound him!")
AND SO SAY BOTH OF US!"

4 Consolidation of power

In the period January 1933 to August 1934, Hitler and the Nazis secured control of all aspects of the German state. By August 1934, Hitler had combined the posts of chancellor and president and was safe in the knowledge that the army supported him. Moreover, the banning of political parties, the control of the media, trade unions and police ensured that there was little or no opposition to the Nazi regime. Once more Hitler pointed out that his actions were always within the legal framework of the time.

The Reichstag fire

The burning down of the Reichstag building only a few weeks after Hitler had become chancellor provided him with the ideal excuse to remove the threat posed by his greatest opposition – the Communist Party.

When Hitler became chancellor, there were only two other Nazis in the cabinet of 12 – Wilhelm Frick and Hermann Goering. Hitler's position was not strong because the Nazis and his allies, the **Nationalist Party**, did not have a majority in the Reichstag. Furthermore, President Hindenburg detested him. However, it was soon clear that von Papen's claim that he would be able to control Hitler was completely wrong.

Hitler immediately called a general election for 5 March 1933, hoping it would give him a clear majority in the Reichstag. If he controlled parliament then he would be able to make the laws needed to tighten his grip on the nation. It would all be done by the rule of law – Nazi law. Violence and terror were again seen in this election campaign and there were about 70 deaths in the weeks leading up to voting day. Once again, Hitler received large amounts of money from leading **industrialists** to assist his campaign. With access to the media, he knew that Goebbels would be able to put the Nazi message over unceasingly. One week before the election, on 27 February 1933, the Reichstag building was set on fire.

ACTIVITY

Work in pairs. Source A shows the Reichstag on fire. What do you think the reactions would be if the Houses of Parliament in London burnt down? Explain your answer carefully. (Think about who people might blame and what people might want the government to do.)

Source A: This photograph shows the Reichstag (German parliament) in flames on the night of 27 February 1933

4 Consolidation of power

It is not known who started the fire, but the Nazis arrested Marinus van der Lubbe, a Dutch communist. Hitler and Goebbels saw this as a great opportunity to exploit and claimed that the communists were about to stage a takeover.

Following the Reichstag fire, Hitler persuaded Hindenburg to sign the 'Decree for the Protection of People and State'. This suspended basic civil rights and allowed the Nazis to imprison large numbers of their political opponents. The communist and **socialist** newspapers were banned.

> **Interpretation 1:** From the memoirs of Rudolf Diels, head of the Prussian Police in 1933. He was writing about Hitler's reaction to the Reichstag fire. Diels was writing in 1950
>
> *Hitler was standing on a balcony gazing at the red ocean of fire. He swang round towards us ... his face had turned quite scarlet with the excitement ... Suddenly he started screaming at the top of his voice: 'Now we'll show them! Anyone who stands in our way will be mown down. The German people have been too soft for too long. Every communist official must be shot. All friends of the communists must be locked up. And that goes for the Social Democrats too.'*

ACTIVITIES

1. Explain why von Papen thought he could control Hitler.
2. Devise captions for Sources A and B for publication in a Nazi newspaper.
3. Carry out some research to find out more about the background and trial of Marinus van der Lubbe.
4. How far does Interpretation 1 support the view that parliamentary democracy had ended in Germany by March 1933?
5. What does Source C show about the role of the police in Berlin in March 1933?

Practice question

Use Source A and your own knowledge to describe the events of the Reichstag fire. (For guidance, see pages 91–92.)

▲ **Source B:** The trial of Marinus van der Lubbe. Van der Lubbe is wearing a striped jacket

▲ **Source C:** Berlin police burn red flags after raiding the homes of communists, 26 March 1933

41

The 1933 election and the Enabling Act

At the election in March 1933, the Nazi Party (**NSDAP**) won 288 seats (see Table 4.1). Despite imprisoning many socialists and communists and having all the advantages of media control, the Nazis did not win a majority of votes. Therefore, a coalition was formed with the National Party, ensuring a majority in the Reichstag. Even though he had a majority, Hitler was disappointed because he needed two-thirds of the seats in order to be able to change the constitution.

Political party	Seats won	Percentage of vote
Nazi Party (NSDAP)	288	43.9
Nationalist Party (DNVP)	52	8.0
People's Party (DVP)	2	1.1
Centre Party (ZP)	92	13.9
Democratic Party (DDP)	5	0.9
Social Democratic Party (SPD)	120	18.3
Communist Party (KPD)	81	12.3
Others	7	1.6

▲ Table 4.1: Election results, March 1933

The importance of the Enabling Act

Hitler's next step was to pass the **Enabling Act.** This would give him and his government full powers for the next four years and would mean that the Reichstag would become a rubber stamp for Nazi activities. The Act was passed – but by devious means (see Figure 4.1).

The Enabling Act was passed on 23 March 1933 and was the end of the Weimar Constitution and democracy. It is regarded as the 'foundation stone' of the Third **Reich** and allowed Hitler to secure closer control of the nation. It quickly resulted in the suspension of civil liberties, the imposition of **censorship** and control of the press, the abolition of **trade unions** and the disbanding of all political parties apart from the Nazi Party. In this way Hitler created a 'dictatorship'.

Figure 4.1: Summary of how Hitler secured votes for the pasing of the Enabling Act

- Communist members not allowed to vote in the chamber.
- SA intimidated members as they entered the chamber.
- Communist Party not counted, thus reducing the overall total and number of votes needed by the Nazis.
- Promises to the Catholic Centre Party won their vote (e.g. no interference in Catholic schools).
- Absentees counted as present.
- **ENABLING BILL PASSED**

ACTIVITY

Work in pairs. You are investigative journalists in 1933 Germany. Write an article exposing the links between the Reichstag fire (pages 42–43) and how the Enabling Act was able to be passed.

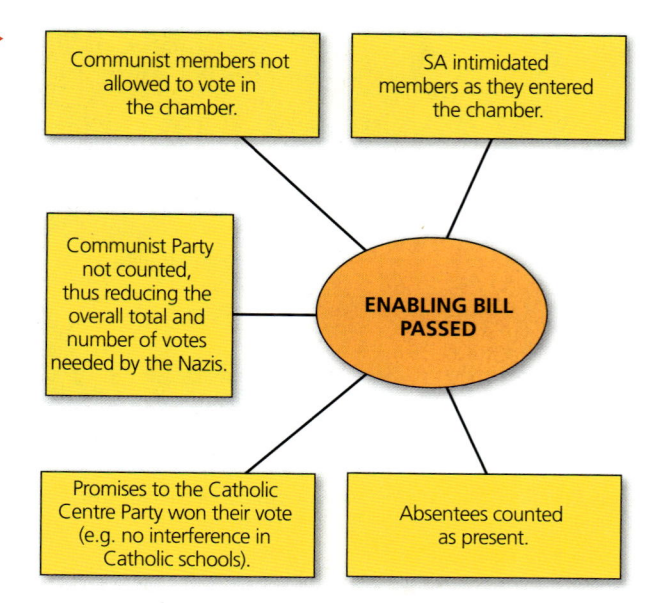

Practice question

Describe how Hitler used the Enabling Act to increase his power. *(For guidance, see page 93.)*

The removal of opposition

With the new Enabling Act, Hitler was now in a position to bring German society into line with Nazi philosophy. This policy was called *Gleichschaltung*. It would create a truly National Socialist state and would mean that every aspect of the social, political and economic life of a German citizen was controlled and monitored by the Nazis.

Trade unions

On 2 May 1933, all trade unions were banned. The Nazis said that a national community had been created, therefore such organisations were no longer needed. The Labour Front (*Deutsche Arbeitsfront* – DAF) was set up to replace not only trade unions but also employers' groups. Wages were decided by the Labour Front and workers received work books which recorded their employment history (see Source D). Employment depended on ownership of the work book. Strikes were outlawed and any dissenters would be sent to the new prisons – concentration camps for political re-education. Some union leaders were sent immediately to the new concentration camps. The first concentration camp opened at Dachau in March 1933. There could be no challenge to the Nazi state.

Political parties

The Communist Party (KPD) had been banned after the Reichstag fire and its property had been confiscated. On 10 May, the Social Democratic Party had its headquarters, property and newspapers seized. The remaining political parties disbanded themselves voluntarily at the end of June and beginning of July. On 14 July 1933 the Law Against the Formation of Parties was passed, which made the Nazi Party the sole legal political party in Germany. Thus within a few months Hitler had achieved political control of the country.

In the November 1933 general election, 95.2 per cent of the electorate voted and the Nazis won 39,638,000 votes. (There was some protest against the Nazis – about 3 million ballot papers were spoilt.)

Control of state government (*Länder*)

Hitler also broke down the federal structure of Germany. There were eighteen *Länder* and each had its own parliament. On occasions in the Weimar period, some of the *Länder* had caused problems for the President because their political make-up differed and they refused to accept decisions made in the Reichstag. President Ebert had issued more than 130 emergency decrees to overrule some of the *Länder*. Hitler decided that the *Länder* were to be run by Reich governors and their parliaments were abolished in January 1934. Thus he centralised the country for the first time since its creation in 1871.

ACTIVITIES

1. What is meant by the term *Gleichschaltung*?
2. How did Hitler increase his control over the German workforce?
3. Explain why Hitler wanted to disband the other political parties.

▼ Source D: The work book of a German worker recording his places of employment between 1932 and 1940. This shows the depth of Nazi control

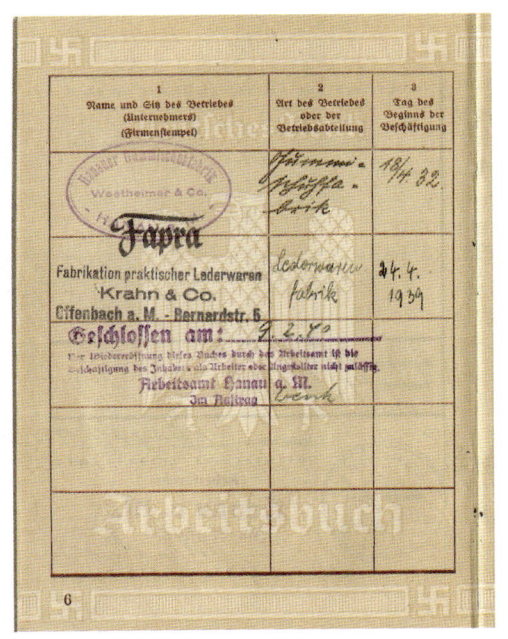

The Night of the Long Knives

The Night of the Long Knives (also known as 'Operation Hummingbird' or 'the Blood Purge') was the purging of Hitler's political and military rivals in the SA (*Sturmabteilung*). One reason for the removal of leaders of the SA was the need to win the support of the army (see page 46). However, in the first months of his chancellorship, Hitler saw the SA as a significant threat.

The SA had been a key part in the growth of the Nazis and by 1933 they were well known across Germany. Most of the SA were working-class people who favoured the socialist views of the Nazi programme. They were hoping that Hitler would introduce reforms to help the workers.

Moreover, Röhm, the leader of the SA, wanted to incorporate the army into the SA and was disappointed by Hitler's close relations with industrialists and the army leaders. Röhm wanted more government interference in the running of the country in order to help the ordinary citizens. He wanted to move away from Germany's class structure and bring greater equality. In effect, he wanted a social revolution. There was further tension for Hitler because his personal bodyguard, the **SS** (**Schutzstaffel**), led by Heinrich Himmler, wished to break away from the SA. Goering (Head of the **Gestapo**) wanted to lead the armed forces and hence saw an opponent in Röhm.

Source E: Hitler and Röhm ▶ with SA troops. The flags are from different SA units across Germany

Source F: From *Hitler Speaks* by H. Rauschning, 1940. Rauschning was a Nazi official who left Germany in 1934 to live in the USA. Here he is describing a conversation with Röhm in 1934. Röhm was drunk

'Adolf's a swine ... He only associates with those on the right ... His old friends aren't good enough for him. Adolf is turning into a gentleman. What he wants is to sit on the hill top and pretend he is God. He knows exactly what I want ... The generals are a lot of old fogeys ... I'm the nucleus of the new army.'

4 Consolidation of power

The events of 30 June 1934

Hitler took action in June, following information from Himmler that Röhm was about to seize power. Hitler now had to make a choice between the SA and the army. He chose the army and on the night of 30 June 1934, Röhm and the main leaders of the SA were shot by members of the SS. Hitler also took the opportunity to settle some old scores – von Schleicher was murdered, as was Gregor Strasser, a key figure among those Nazis with socialist views similar to Röhm's. About 400 people were murdered in the purge.

> **Source G:** From Hitler's speech to the Reichstag on 13 July 1934, justifying his actions concerning the SA
>
> *In the circumstances I had to make but one decision. If disaster was to be prevented at all, action had to be taken with lightning speed. Only a ruthless and bloody intervention might still perhaps stifle the spread of revolt. If anyone reproaches me and asks why I did not resort to the regular courts of justice for conviction of the offenders, then all I can say is – 'In this hour I was responsible for the fate of the German people and therefore I became the supreme judge of the German people.'*

The impact of the Night of the Long Knives

The Night of the Long Knives is often seen as the turning point for Hitler's rule in Germany. He eradicated would-be opponents and secured the support of the army. The SA was relegated to a minor role and, if there had been any doubt about Hitler's rule, it was now clear that fear and terror would play significant roles.

▲ **Source H:** A cartoon by David Low, which appeared in the *London Evening Standard*, 3 July 1934. The caption reads: 'They salute with both hands now.' Goering is standing to Hitler's right, dressed as a Viking hero, and Goebbels is on his knees behind Hitler. The paper at the feet of the SA has the words 'Hitler's unkept promises', and the swastika on Hitler's armband is between the words 'the double cross'

ACTIVITIES

1. Study Source E. What does it show you about Hitler and the SA?
2. Explain why Hitler was becoming concerned about the role of the SA.
3. Study Source G. How does Hitler justify the Night of the Long Knives?
4. How important was the Night of the Long Knives in increasing Hitler's power?

Practice questions

1. What was the purpose of Source H? (For guidance, see pages 94–95.)
2. Study Sources F (page 44) and G. Which of the sources is more useful to an historian studying the reasons for the Night of the Long Knives? (For guidance, see pages 96–97.)

Hitler becomes *Führer*

By the end of August 1934 Hitler had become the sole ruler of Germany, combining the roles of chancellor and president and giving himself the title of **Führer**.

However, first Hitler had to ensure the support of the army. By early 1934, there were some in the Nazi Party, such as Röhm, the leader of the SA, who wished to incorporate it into the SA. However, Hitler knew that there would be opposition from the generals and this could mean a challenge to his own position. Furthermore, if he removed the SA, he could win the support of the army in his bid for the presidency. The army felt threatened by the SA and many of the army leaders did not like the socialist nature of the SA. President Hindenburg was becoming very frail and Hitler sought to combine his own post and that of president. The support of the army was gained following the Night of the Long Knives when the leaders of the SA were assassinated.

Following the death of Hindenburg in August 1934, the army swore allegiance to Hitler who, having combined the roles of chancellor and president, was now their *Führer* (see Source I). He became the Commander-in-Chief of the Armed Forces. Hitler decided he needed to seek the approval of the German people when he combined the posts. In the referendum of 19 August, more than 90 per cent of the voters (38 million) agreed with his action. Only 4.5 million voted against him and 870,000 spoiled their ballot papers.

> **Source I:** The army's oath of allegiance to Hitler, August 1934
>
> *I swear before God to give my unconditional obedience to Adolf Hitler, Führer of the Reich and of the German people, and I pledge my word as a brave soldier to observe this oath always, even at the peril of my life.*

ACTIVITIES

1. Study Sources I and J. What do they show about the support for Hitler in August 1934?
2. How did Hitler increase his control over Germany after the death of President Hindenburg?
3. Explain why Hitler needed the support of the army.

Practice question

Was the passing of the Enabling Law the most important event in Hitler's consolidation of power between 1933 and 1934? *Use your own knowledge and understanding of the issue to support your answer. (For guidance, see pages 98–99.)*

▲ **Source J: Hitler Youth** on the occasion of the Referendum on the Merging of the Offices of Reich President and Reich chancellor (19 August 1934). The words on the side of the lorry read 'The *Führer* commands, we follow! Everyone say Yes!'

5 Nazi economic, social and racial policy

In the years 1933–39 the Nazis introduced policies that reflected their own beliefs about the role of various groups in Germany. Women reverted to their traditional family role and the young were indoctrinated into Nazi ideas. The economy was reorganised to prepare Germany for war and eliminate unemployment. Moreover, the Nazis ensured control of everyday life by controlling religion, education, the family and working people. Finally, the Jews were persecuted in order to drive them out of Germany.

Attempts to reduce unemployment

By January 1933, when Hitler became Chancellor, Germany had experienced more than three years of **depression** with unemployment reaching 6 million. Hitler had appealed to the unemployed and promised to create jobs if he was elected. On becoming chancellor, he introduced a series of measures to reduce unemployment.

The National Labour Service Corps (*Reichsarbeitsdienst*, RAD)

This was a scheme to provide young men with manual labour jobs. From 1935 it was compulsory for all men aged 18–25 to serve in the **RAD** for six months. In 1939, the RAD was extended to women. It was intended to 'educate German youth in the spirit of National Socialism and to acquire a true conception of work, above all a respect for manual labour'.

Workers lived in Labour Service camps, wore uniforms, received very low pay and carried out military drills as well as work (see Source A).

Source A: An Austrian visitor describes a National Labour Service camp in 1938

The camps are organised on thoroughly military lines. The youths wear uniforms like soldiers. The only difference is that they carry spades instead of rifles and work in the fields.

ACTIVITIES

1. What do Sources A and B suggest about the methods used by the Nazis to reduce unemployment?
2. What was the purpose of the RAD organisation?

◀ **Source B:** Young men in the National Labour Service Corps carrying out a military drill in 1933

47

Job creation schemes

At first Hitler spent millions on job creation schemes, with costs rising from 18.4 billion Reichsmarks in 1933 to 37.1 billion five years later. The Nazis subsidised private firms, especially in the construction industry. They also introduced a massive road-building programme to provide Germany with 7,000 km of *autobahns* (motorways), as well as other public works schemes, such as the construction of hospitals, schools and houses.

Source C: An official Nazi photograph showing workers gathering to begin work on the first *autobahn*, September 1933

Invisible unemployment

The Nazis used some dubious methods to keep down the unemployment figures. The official figures did not include the following:

- Jews dismissed from their jobs
- unmarried men under 25 who were pushed into National Labour Service schemes
- women dismissed from their jobs or who gave up work to get married
- opponents of the Nazi regime held in concentration camps.

The official figures also listed part-time workers as being fully employed and by 1939, only 35,000 male workers were listed as unemployed out of a workforce of 25 million.

Rearmament

Hitler was determined to build up the armed forces in readiness for future war. This, in turn, greatly reduced unemployment.

- The reintroduction of **conscription** in 1935 took thousands of young men into military service. The army grew from 100,000 in 1933 to 1,400,000 by 1939.
- Heavy industry expanded to meet the needs of rearmament. Coal and chemical usage doubled in the years 1933 to 1939; oil, iron and steel usage trebled.
- Billions were spent producing tanks, aircraft and ships. In 1933, 3.5 billion marks were spent on rearmament. This figure had increased to 26 billion marks by 1939.

Practice question

What was the purpose of Source C? *(For guidance, see pages 94–95.)*

ACTIVITIES

1. How successful was Hitler in reducing unemployment in Germany between 1933 and 1939?
2. How accurate are Nazi claims that their policies led to a dramatic fall in the number of unemployed in Germany?

5 Nazi economic, social and racial policy

Nazi policy towards workers

The Nazis were determined to control the workforce to prevent the possibility of strikes and to ensure that industry met the needs of rearmament. This was achieved through two organisations, the German Labour Front and Strength through Joy.

The German Labour Front (*Deutsche Arbeitsfront*, DAF)

On 2 May 1933, to avoid the possibility of strikes and other industrial action, the Nazis banned all trade unions. They were replaced by the German Labour Front under its leader, Robert Ley. The DAF became the largest organisation in Nazi Germany and had 22 million members by 1939.

- The DAF included employers and workers and was supposed to represent the interests of both.
- All strikes were banned and wages were decided by the Labour Front.
- Workers were given relatively high wages, job security, and social and leisure programmes.
- Workers received work books which recorded their employment history. Employment depended on ownership of a work book (see Source E on page 43).
- In theory DAF membership was voluntary, but any worker in any area of German commerce or industry would have found it hard to get a job without being a member.
- The membership fee for the Labour Front ranged from 15 pfennig to 3 Reichsmarks depending on the occupation of the worker.

Volkswagen scheme

In 1938, the German Labour Front organised the Volkswagen (people's car) scheme, giving workers an opportunity to subscribe five marks a week to buy their own car. It was stated by the Labour Front that, when complete, the factory would produce more cars per year than Ford in the USA. By the end of 1938, more than 150,000 people had ordered a car and they were told to expect delivery in 1940.

This was a swindle. Not a single customer took delivery of a car because production was shifted to military vehicles in 1939. None of the money that had been contributed was refunded.

ACTIVITIES

1. What was the purpose of the Volkswagen scheme?
2. Study Source D. Why was this photograph displayed all over Germany?

Practice question

Describe how the German Labour Front (DAF) was used to help reduce unemployment. *(For guidance, see page 93.)*

▼ **Source D:** Volkswagens at Factory Dedication, May 1938

Strength through Joy (*Kraft durch Freude* – KdF)

This was an organisation set up by the German Labour Front to replace **trade unions**. The KdF tried to improve the leisure time of German workers by sponsoring a wide range of leisure and cultural trips. These included concerts, theatre visits, museum tours, sporting events, weekend trips, holidays and cruises. Cruises went to the Canary Islands, Madeira and the Norwegian Fiords, and cheap holidays were offered in Italy. About 10 million people went on KdF holidays in Germany in 1938. All were provided at a low cost, giving ordinary workers access to activities normally reserved for the better off.

Beauty of Work (*Schönheit der Arbeit*) was a department of the KdF that tried to improve working conditions. It organised the building of canteens, swimming pools and sports facilities. It also installed better lighting in the workplace.

▲ Figure 5.1: Official figures from the Nazi Party showing numbers taking part in KdF activities in 1938

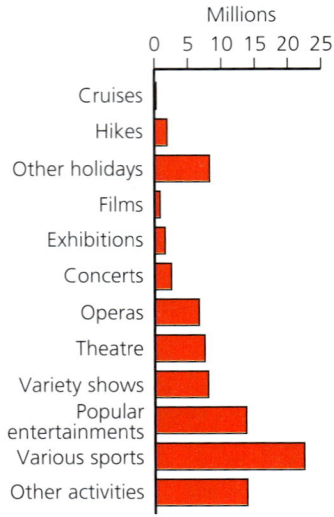

Source F: Extract from the magazine *Strength through Joy*, 1936

KdF is now running weekly theatre trips to Munich from the countryside. Special theatre trains are coming to Munich on weekdays from as far away as 120 km. So a lot of our comrades who used to be in the Outdoor Club, for example, are availing themselves of the opportunity of going on trips with KdF. There is simply no other choice. Walking trips have also become very popular.

ACTIVITY ?

How useful are Source F and Figure 5.1 to an historian studying the work of the KDF?

Source E: ▶ A Strength through Joy poster of 1938 encouraging German workers to go on cruises

5 Nazi economic, social and racial policy

The role of women

Women had made significant progress in their position in German society during the 1920s, as shown in the Table 5.1.

Political progress	Economic progress	Social progress
Women over the age of 20 were given the vote and took an increasing interest in politics. By 1933 one-tenth of the members of the Reichstag were female.	Many women took up careers in the professions, especially the civil service, law, medicine and teaching. Those who worked in the civil service earned the same as men. By 1933 there were 100,000 women teachers and 3,000 doctors.	Socially, women went out unescorted, drank and smoked in public, were frequently slim and fashion conscious. They often wore relatively short skirts, had their hair cut short and wore make-up.

▲ Table 5.1: Progress made by German women in the 1920s

Nazi ideals

The Nazis had a very traditional view of the role of women, which was very different from women's position in society in the 1920s. According to the Nazi ideal, a woman:

- did not wear make-up
- was blonde, heavy-hipped and athletic
- wore flat shoes and a full skirt
- did not smoke
- did not go out to work
- did all the household duties, especially cooking and bringing up the children
- took no interest in politics.

◀ Source I: A Nazi poster of 1937 showing the ideal image of a German woman. The German translates as 'Support the cause – mother and child'

Source G: Goebbels describes the role of women in a speech in 1929

The mission of women is to be beautiful and to bring children into the world. The female bird pretties herself for her mate and hatches eggs for him. In exchange, the male takes care of gathering the food and stands guard and wards off the enemy.

Source H: A German rhyme addressed to women

Take hold of the kettle, broom and pan,
Then you'll surely get a man!
Shop and office leave alone,
Your true life work lies at home.

ACTIVITY

1 What do Sources G and H suggest about Nazi attitudes towards the role of women?

Practice question

What was the purpose of Source I? *(For guidance, see pages 94–95.)*

Changes under the Nazis

The Nazis brought in a series of measures to change the role of women.

Marriage and family

The Nazis were very worried by the decline in the birth rate. In 1900 there had been more than 2 million live births per year but this figure dropped to less than 1 million in 1933.

- A massive propaganda campaign was launched to promote motherhood and large families.
- In 1933 the Law for the Encouragement of Marriage was introduced. This aimed to increase Germany's falling birth rate by giving loans to help young couples to marry, provided the wife left her job. Couples were allowed to keep one-quarter of the loan for each child born, up to four children.
- On Hitler's mother's birthday (12 August) medals, called the Mother's Cross, were awarded to women with large families.
- In 1938 the Nazis changed the divorce law – a divorce was possible if a husband or wife could not have children. A childless marriage was seen as worthless by the Nazis.
- The Nazis also set up the *Lebensborn* (Life Springs) programme whereby specially chosen unmarried women could 'donate a baby to the **Führer**' by becoming pregnant by 'racially pure' **SS** (*Schutzstaffel*) men.
- A new national organisation, the German Women's Enterprise, organised classes and radio talks on household topics and the skills of motherhood.

> **Interpretation 1:** Marianne Gartner was a member of the League of German Maidens and remembers one of its meetings in 1936
>
> *At one meeting the team leader raised her voice. 'There is no greater honour for a German woman than to bear children for the Führer and for the Fatherland! The Führer has ruled that no family will be complete without at least four children. A German woman does not use make-up! A German woman does not smoke! She has a duty to keep herself fit and healthy! Any questions?' 'Why isn't the Führer married and a father himself?' I asked.*

▲ **Source J:** A German cartoon from the 1930s. Translated, the caption reads 'Introducing Frau Müller who up to now has brought 12 children into the world'

1. Remember that you are a German.
2. If you are genetically healthy, you should get married.
3. Keep your body pure.
4. Keep your mind and spirit pure.
5. **Marry only for love.**
6. As a German choose only a husband of similar or related blood.
7. In choosing a husband, ask about his ancestors.
8. Health is essential for physical beauty.
9. Don't look for a playmate but for a companion in marriage.
10. You should want to have as many children as possible.

▲ **Source K:** An artist's interpretation of a Nazi pamphlet sent to young German women

5 Nazi economic, social and racial policy

Work

Instead of going to work, women were asked to stick to the 'three Ks': *Kinder, Küche, Kirche* – 'children, kitchen, church'. The Nazis had another incentive to get women to give up work. They had been elected partly because they promised more jobs. Every job left by a woman returning to the home became available for a man. Women doctors, civil servants and teachers were forced to leave their jobs. Schoolgirls were trained for work at home (see pages 55–56) and discouraged from going on to higher education.

However, from 1937 the Nazis had to reverse these policies. Germany was rearming. Men were joining the army. Now the Nazis needed more women to go out to work. They abolished the marriage loans and introduced a compulsory 'duty year' for all women entering employment. This usually meant helping on a farm or in a family home in return for bed and board but no pay. This change of policy was not very successful. By 1939, there were fewer women working than there had been under the Weimar Republic.

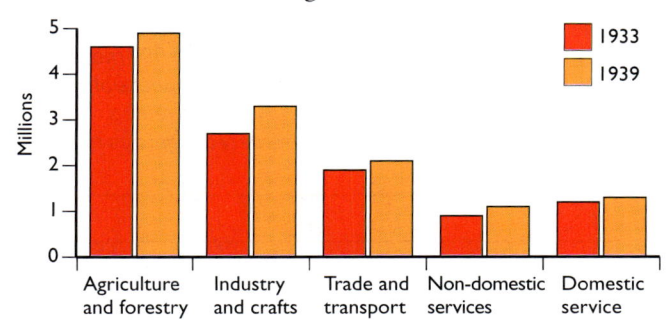

▲ Figure 5.2: Employment of women (millions)

Appearance

Women were encouraged to keep healthy and wear their hair in a bun or plaits. They were discouraged from wearing trousers, high heels and make-up, from dyeing or styling their hair, and from slimming, as this was seen as bad for childbearing.

ACTIVITIES

1. Construct two mind maps showing how the position of women changed from the Weimar into the Nazi Period.
   - ☐ Label the first mind map with the features of 'modern women' during Weimar Germany.
   - ☐ Label the second mind map 'Nazi attitudes to women'.
2. How far does Interpretation 1 support the view that women occupied an important place in Nazi society?
3. What message is the cartoonist trying to put across in Source J?
4. What use is Source K to an historian studying Nazi attitudes to women?
5. Design a mind map like the one below to show the expectations for women living in Germany during the time of the Nazis. The first box has been completed for you.

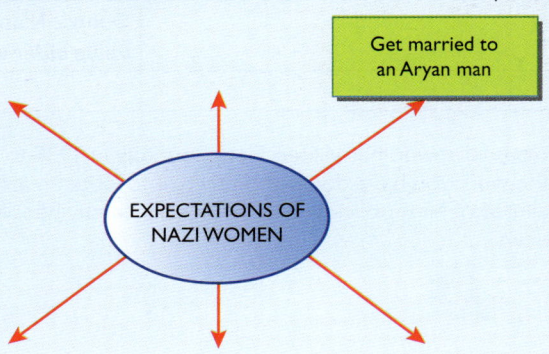

   Get married to an Aryan man

   EXPECTATIONS OF NAZI WOMEN

Practice question

Describe how the Nazis viewed the role of women. *(For guidance, see page 93.)*

53

WJEC GCSE History: Germany in Transition, 1919–39 and the USA: A Nation of Contrasts, 1910–29

How successful were these policies?

By looking carefully at the sources below and answering the activity questions you will be able to make your own mind up as to whether Nazi policies towards women had any success.

Source L: Extract from a letter from several women to a Leipzig newspaper in 1934

Today man is educated not for, but against, marriage. We see our daughters growing up in stupid aimlessness living only in a vague hope of getting a man and having children. A son, even the youngest, laughs in his mother's face. He regards her as his servant and women in general are merely willing tools of his aims.

Source M: From a newspaper article by Judith Grunfeld, an American journalist, 1937

*How many women workers did the Führer send home? According to the statistics of the German Department of Labour, there were in June 1936, 5,470,000 employed women, or 1,200,000 more than in January 1933. The Nazi campaign has not been successful in reducing the numbers of women employed. It has simply squeezed them out of better paid positions into the **sweated trades**. This type of labour with its miserable wages and long hours is extremely dangerous to the health of women and degrades the family.*

Interpretation 2: The memories of Wilhelmine Haferkamp who was 22 in 1933. She lived in the industrial city of Oberhausen

When one had ten children, well not ten but a pile of them, one had to join the Nazi Party. 1933 it was and I already had three children and the fourth on the way. When 'child-rich' people were in the Party the children had a great chance to advance. I got 30 marks per child from the Hitler government and 20 marks per child from the city. That was a lot of money. I sometimes got more 'child money' than my husband earned.

Source N: From a newspaper article by Toni Christen, an American journalist, 1939

I talked to Mrs Schmidt, a woman of about 50, as she came out of the shop. 'You see, older women are no good in Germany,' she said. 'We are no longer capable of bearing children. We have no value to the state. They don't care for us mothers or grandmothers any more. We are worn out, discarded.'

ACTIVITIES

1. Make a copy of the following table. Sort Sources L, M, N, and Interpretation 2 into successes and failures for Nazi policies in the areas of marriage/family and jobs. Complete the table with an explanation of your choices. One has been done for you.

	Success	Failure
Marriage/family		Source N as the Nazis did not value older women
Jobs		

2. You are a British journalist who has visited Nazi Germany in 1938 to investigate the role of women. Use the work you have done on Activity 1 to write an article explaining the successes and failures of Nazi policies. You will need a catchy headline. You could include imaginary interviews.

5 Nazi economic, social and racial policy

Controlling education

Hitler saw the young as the future of the Third **Reich**. They had to be converted to the Nazi ideals. This was achieved through control of education. Everyone in Germany had to go to school until the age of fourteen. After that schooling was optional. Boys and girls went to separate schools. Figure 5.3 gives an overview of school life in Nazi Germany.

▼ Figure 5.3: How Nazis controlled schools after 1933

TEXTBOOKS

These were rewritten to fit the Nazi view of history and racial purity. All textbooks had to be approved by the Ministry of Education. *Mein Kampf* became a standard text.

TEACHERS

School teachers had to swear an oath of loyalty to Hitler and join the **Nazi Teachers' League**. By 1937, 97 per cent of teachers had joined. Teachers had to promote Nazi ideals in the classroom and many were dismissed if they did not show that they were committed to Nazism. By 1936, 36 per cent of teachers were members of the Nazi Party.

LESSONS

These began and ended with the students saluting and saying **'Heil Hitler'**. Nazi themes were presented through every subject. Maths problems dealt with social issues. Geography lessons were used to show how Germany was surrounded by hostile neighbours. In history lessons, students were taught about the evils of communism and the severity of the Treaty of Versailles.

CURRICULUM

Under the Nazis the school curriculum was changed to prepare students for their future roles. Hitler wanted healthy, fit men and women so 15 per cent of time was devoted to physical education. With the boys the emphasis was on preparation for the military. There was also great emphasis on Germany's past and the **Aryan** race. Students were taught that Aryans were superior and should not marry inferior races such as Jews. Girls took needlework and home crafts, especially cookery, to become good homemakers and mothers. New subjects such as race studies were introduced to put across Nazi ideas on race and population control. Children were taught how to measure their skulls and to classify racial types. Religious education became optional.

Source O: A question from a maths textbook, 1933

The Jews are aliens in Germany. In 1933 there were 66,060,000 inhabitants of the German Reich of whom 499,862 were Jews. What is the percentage of aliens in Germany?

Interpretation 3: From the memoirs, written in the 1960s, of a German who was a student in the 1930s

No one in our class ever read Mein Kampf. *I myself only used the book for quotations. In general we didn't do much about Nazi ideas. Anti-Semitism wasn't mentioned much by our teachers except through Richard Wagner's essay 'The Jews in Music'. We did, however, do a lot of physical education and cookery.*

ACTIVITIES

1. Explain why the Nazis wanted to control education.
2. Study Source O. What does it show you about education in Nazi Germany?
3. What can you infer from Interpretation 3 about education in Nazi Germany?

Practice question

Describe how the school curriculum changed under the Nazis. *(For guidance, see page 93.)*

WJEC GCSE History: Germany in Transition, 1919–39 and the USA: A Nation of Contrasts, 1910–29

The Hitler Youth movement

The Nazis also wanted to control the spare time of the young. This was achieved through the **Hitler Youth**. Young people had to be converted to Nazi ideals such as obedience, following the *Führer*, placing the nation first and strengthening the racial purity of the nation. If young people were indoctrinated in their leisure time, in the Hitler Youth, as well as through schooling and education, they would become loyal and committed followers of Hitler and would not want to criticise the Nazi way of life. Therefore:

- All other youth organisations were banned.
- From 1939 membership of the Hitler Youth was compulsory.
- By 1939 there were 7 million members.

Hitler Youth males	Hitler Youth females
▲ **Source P:** A recruiting poster for the Hitler Youth, 1933, which says in the poster 'Come to us!' and at the foot: 'Join the Hitler Youth'	▲ **Source Q:** A recruiting poster for the Young Girls which says 'Every ten-year-old to us'
Boys joined the German Young People (Jungvolk) at the age of ten. From fourteen to eighteen they were members of the Hitler Youth (HitlerJugend). They learned Nazi songs and ideas and took part in athletics, hiking and camping. As they got older they practised marching, map reading and military skills. Many enjoyed the comradeship. It is also possible they enjoyed the fact that their camps were often near to those of the League of German Maidens.	*Girls joined the Young Girls (Jungmädel) at the age of ten. From fourteen to eighteen they were members of the League of German Maidens (Bund Deutsche Mädchen). They did much the same as the boys except they also learned domestic skills in preparation for motherhood and marriage. There was much less emphasis on military training.*

Practice questions

1. Use Source P and your own knowledge to describe the Hitler Youth movement. *(For guidance, see pages 91–92.)*
2. Describe the activities of the Hitler Youth movement. *(For guidance, see page 93.)*

ACTIVITY

1. What do Sources P and Q suggest about the Hitler Youth movement?

5 Nazi economic, social and racial policy

How successful were these policies?

Although many young Germans joined the Hitler Youth, it was not popular with some of its members.

Interpretation 4: The memories of a Hitler Youth leader given during an interview in the 1980s

What I liked about the Hitler Youth was the comradeship. I was full of enthusiasm when I joined the Young People at the age of ten. I can still remember how deeply moved I was when I heard the club mottoes: 'Young People are hard. They can keep a secret. They are loyal. They are comrades.' And then there were the trips! Is anything nicer than enjoying the splendours of the homeland in the company of one's comrades?

Source R: From an article on the Hitler Youth published in a British magazine in 1938

There seems little enthusiasm for the Hitler Youth, with membership falling. Many no longer want to be commanded, but wish to do as they like. Usually only a third of a group appears for roll-call. At evening meetings it is a great event if 20 turn up out of 80, but usually there are only about 10 or 12.

Source S: A letter written by a member of the Hitler Youth to his parents in 1936

How did we live in Camp S—, which is supposed to be an example to all the camps? We practically didn't have a minute of the day to ourselves. This isn't camp life, no sir! It's military barrack life! Drill starts right after a meagre breakfast. We would like to have athletics but there isn't any. Instead we have military exercises, down in the mud, till the tongue hangs out of your mouth. And we have only one wish: sleep, sleep …

ACTIVITIES

1. Explain why some teenagers rebelled against the Hitler Youth Movement.
2. How useful are Interpretation 4 and Source R to an historian studying the Hitler Youth movement?
3. Using Source S explain why the Hitler Youth movement was not popular with all young Germans.
4. Do Sources R–T and Interpretation 4 suggest that Nazi policies were popular with the young? To answer this question make a copy of the table and complete it. One example has been done for you. Give a brief explanation for each decision.

Popular	Unpopular	Undecided
		Source S because although it shows a march, the girls do not look enthusiastic.

▼ **Source T:** Members of the League of German Maidens going on a hike, 1936

Attitudes to religion

Nazi ideals were opposed to the beliefs and values of the Christian Church.

Nazism	Christianity
Glorified strength and violence	Teaches love and forgiveness
Despised the weak	Helps the weak
Believed in racial superiority	Respect for all people
Saw Hitler as god-like figure	Belief in God

However, Hitler could not immediately persecute Christianity as Germany was essentially a Christian country. Almost two-thirds of the population was Protestant, most of whom lived in the north; almost one-third was Catholic, most of whom lived in the south.

Hitler set up a Ministry of Church Affairs in 1935 in an attempt to weaken the hold the Catholic and Protestant churches had on the people. In addition to the ministry, the German Faith Movement was encouraged by the Nazis, in the hope of replacing Christian values and ceremonies with pagan (non-Christian) ideas. However, only about 5 per cent of the population joined it.

▲ Figure 5.4: Symbol of the German Faith Movement

ACTIVITIES

1. Suggest reasons why the symbol of the German Faith Movement (Figure 5.4) was so designed.
2. Eventually Hitler would have completely removed the Christian Churches and replaced them with a Nazi Church. Who or what would have taken the place of the following:
   - God
   - the Bible
   - the cross as a symbol
   - the disciples?
3. Suggest reasons why Sources U and V are anti-Catholic.

The Catholic Church

Despite the fact that many Catholics supported Hitler because of his opposition to Communism, Hitler saw the Catholic Church as a threat to his Nazi state:

- Catholics owed their first allegiance not to Hitler but to the Pope. They had divided loyalties. Hitler said a person was either a Christian or a German but not both.
- There were Catholic schools and youth organisations whose message to the young was at odds with that of the Nazi Party.
- The Catholics consistently supported the Centre Party. Hitler intended to remove this party (the party dissolved itself in early July 1933).

> **Source U:** From police reports in Bavaria in 1937 and 1938
>
> *The influence of the Catholic Church on the population is so strong that the Nazi spirit cannot penetrate. The local population is ever under the strong influence of the priests. These people prefer to believe what the priests say from the pulpit than the words of the best Nazi speakers.*

At first, however, Hitler decided to co-operate with the Catholic Church. In July 1933, he signed a **concordat** or agreement with Pope Pius XI. The Pope agreed that the Catholic Church would stay out of politics if Hitler agreed not to interfere with the Church. Within a few months Hitler had broken this agreement.

- Priests were harassed and arrested. Many criticised the Nazis and ended up in concentration camps.
- Catholic schools were interfered with and eventually abolished.
- Catholic youth movements closed down.
- Monasteries were closed.

> **Source V:** From a letter written by Cardinal Bertram to the Vatican, 10 September 1933. Bertram was also the Archbishop of Breslau
>
> *Parents no longer want to let their children belong to Catholic organisations because of pressure from the subordinate parts of the Nazi Party ... and everywhere teachers are under pressure to direct children to the Hitler Youth. On all sides, Catholic associations are being accused of political unreliability, of lack of patriotism and of enmity against the state.*

5 Nazi economic, social and racial policy

The Protestant Church

There were some Protestants who admired Hitler. They were called 'German Christians'. They established a new Reich Church, hoping to combine all Protestants under one Church. Their leader was Ludwig Müller who became the *Reich* bishop, which means national leader, in September 1933.

> **Source W:** A Protestant pastor speaking in a 'German Christian' church in 1937
>
> *We all know that if the Third Reich were to collapse today, Communism would come in its place. Therefore we must show loyalty to the Führer who has saved us from Communism and given us a better future. Support the 'German Christian' Church.*

However, many Protestants opposed Nazism, which they believed conflicted greatly with their own Christian beliefs. They were led by Pastor Martin Niemöller, a First World War submarine commander. In December 1933 they set up the Pastors' Emergency League for those who opposed Hitler.

ACTIVITIES

1. Study Source W. This speech was widely publicised by the Nazis. Why?
2. Study Source X. You are an opponent of the new Reich Protestant Church. Devise a caption for this photograph.

Practice questions

1. Use Source Y and your own knowledge to describe Nazi attempts to control the Church. *(For guidance on how to answer this type of question, see pages 91–92.)*
2. Describe the Nazi policies towards the Church in Germany. *(For guidance see page 93.)*

▲ **Source X:** A photograph of Reich bishop Müller after the consecration of the Gustav-Adolf Church, Berlin, 1933

▲ **Source Y:** A poster by John Heartfield, a communist artist who opposed the Nazis. Hitler is shown nailing swastika arms to the Christian cross held by Jesus. The words translate to 'The cross wasn't heavy enough'

The treatment of the Jews

Central to Nazi policy was the creation of a pure German state. This meant treating all non-German groups, especially the Jews, as second-class citizens. Hitler's theory of race was based on the idea of the 'master race' and the 'subhumans' (*Untermenschen*). He tried to back up this theory by saying that the Bible showed there were only two races – the Jews and the Aryans – and that God had a special purpose for the Aryans.

The Nazis believed that the Germans were a pure race of Aryan descent – from the *Herrenvolk* or 'master race'. They were shown in art as blond, blue-eyed, tall, lean and athletic – a people fit to master the world. However, this race had been contaminated by the 'subhumans'.

Jews and Slavs on the other hand were the 'subhumans'. Nazi propaganda portrayed Jews as evil moneylenders. Hitler regarded the Jews as an evil force and was convinced of their involvement in a world conspiracy to destroy civilisation.

Hitler believed that Germany's future was dependent on the creation of a pure Aryan racial state. This would be achieved by:

- selective breeding
- destroying the Jews.

Selective breeding meant preventing anyone who did not conform to the Aryan type from having children. The SS were part of the drive for selective breeding. They recruited men who were of Aryan blood, tall, fair-haired and blue-eyed. They were only allowed to marry women of Aryan blood.

◀ **Source Z:** A poster from an exhibition, used by the Nazis to turn people against the Jews, with the caption 'The Eternal Jew'

Source AA: From a speech given by Hitler to Nazi supporters in 1922

There can be no compromise. There are only two possibilities. Either victory of the Aryan Master Race or the wiping out of the Aryan and the victory of the Jew.

ACTIVITY

What were the main features of Nazi racial theory?

Practice question

What was the purpose of Source Z? *(For guidance, see pages 94–95.)*

5 Nazi economic, social and racial policy

The persecution of the Jews

Hitler and the Nazi Party were by no means the first to think of the Jews as different and treat them with hostility as outsiders. **Anti-Semitism** goes back to the Middle Ages. Figure 5.4 gives an overview of why the Jews were persecuted.

Why were the Jews persecuted?

- Jewish people have been persecuted throughout history, for example in England during the Middle Ages. This is because Jewish people stood out as different in regions across Europe. They had a different religion and different customs. Some Christians blamed the Jews for the execution of Christ and argued that Jews should be punished forever. Some Jews became moneylenders and became quite wealthy. This increased resentment and suspicion from people who owed them money or were jealous of their success.

- Hitler had spent several years in Vienna where there was a long tradition of anti-Semitism.

  He lived as a down and out and resented the wealth of many of the Viennese Jews. In the 1920s he used the Jews as scapegoats for all society's problems.

  He blamed them for Germany's defeat in the First World War, hyperinflation in 1923 and the Depression of 1929.

- Hitler was determined to create a 'pure' racial state. This did not include the 500,000 Jews who were living in Germany. He wanted to eliminate the Jews from German society. He had no master plan for achieving this, however, and until the beginning of the Second World War; a great deal of Nazi Jewish policy was uncoordinated.

▲ Figure 5.4: Reasons for the persecution of the Jews

Source BB: From *Mein Kampf* written by Hitler in 1924

Was there any form of filth or crime without at least one Jew involved in it? If you cut continuously into such a sore, you find, like a maggot in a rotting body, often dazzled by the light – a Jew.

◀ **Source CC:** A Nazi cartoon of the early 1930s. Translated, the title reads 'Jewish department store octopus'

ACTIVITIES

1. Use Source BB and your own knowledge to explain why Hitler saw the Jews as the enemy of Germany.
2. Study Source CC. Why was the cartoon published in the early 1930s?
3. Explain why the Nazis persecuted the Jews.

Anti-Semitism in schools

The persecution of the Jews did not begin immediately. Hitler needed to ensure that he had the support of most of the German people for his anti-Semitic policies. This was achieved through propaganda and the use of schools. Young people especially were encouraged to hate Jews, with school lessons and textbooks putting across anti-Semitic views.

School textbooks and teaching materials were controlled by the Ministry of Education. The government was able to put anti-Semitic material into every classroom. In addition, laws were passed to restrict Jewish people's involvement in education. In October 1936 Jewish teachers were forbidden to give private tuition to German students. In November 1938 Jewish children were expelled from German schools.

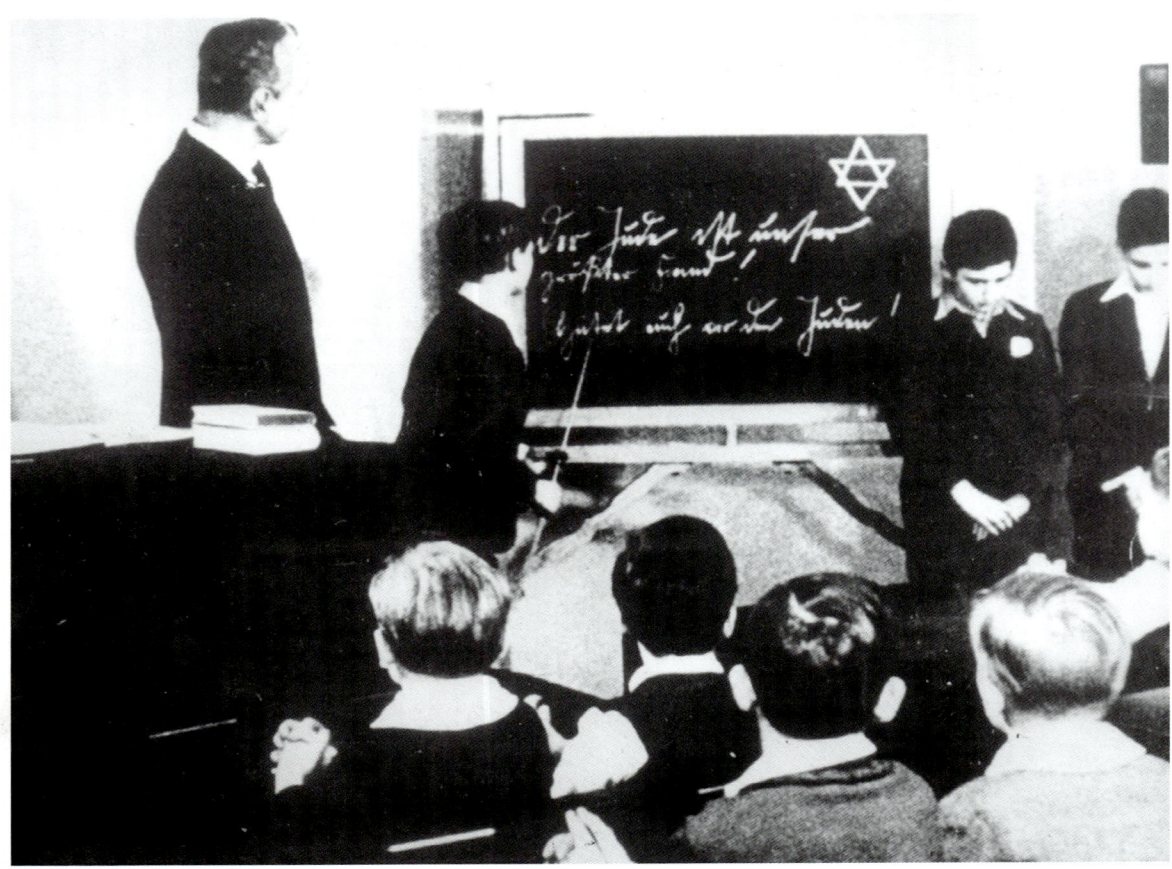

▲ **Source DD:** Jewish schoolchildren being humiliated in front of their class. The writing on the board reads 'The Jews are our greatest enemy!' and 'Beware of the Jews!'

Interpretation 5: From the memoirs of a German mother, written after the Second World War, *Germany 1918–45* by J. Brooman (Longman, 1996)

One day my daughter came home humiliated. 'It was not so nice today.' 'What happened?' I asked. The teacher had sent the Aryan children to one side of the classroom, and the non-Aryans to the other. Then the teacher told the Aryans to study the appearance of the others and to point out the marks of their Jewish race. They stood separated as if by a gulf, children who had played together as friends the day before.

Interpretation 6: An extract from the textbook *Germany 1918–45* by R. Radway (Hodder, 1998)

Inge sits in the doctor's waiting room. Again and again her mind dwells on the warnings of the BDM leader: 'A German must not consult a Jewish doctor! And particularly not a German girl! Many a girl who has gone to a Jewish doctor to be cured has found disease and disgrace. The door opens. Inge looks in. There stands the Jew. She screams. She's so frightened she drops the magazine. Her eyes stare into the Jewish doctor's face. His face is the face of the devil. In the middle of the devil's face is a huge crooked nose. Behind the spectacles two criminal eyes. And thick lips that are grinning. 'Now, I've got you at last, a little German girl.'

ACTIVITIES

1. Study Source DD. What does it show you about the treatment of Jewish schoolchildren?
2. How useful are Interpretations 5 and 6 to an historian studying how education was used to encourage hatred of the Jews?
3. How did life change for Jewish children under the Nazis?

5 Nazi economic, social and racial policy

Measures taken against the Jews

Persecution of the Jews in the 1930s was irregular. Initially there was the economic boycott, which was not well supported and disliked by many Germans. Then legal and open discrimination increased in the years to 1936 but diminished during the Olympics. Persecution then increased with further legislation and **Kristallnacht** (see page 64). Increased numbers of Jews had left Germany by the end of the decade. Figure 5.5 below summarises the different measures taken against the Jews.

◀ Figure 5.5: The different measures taken against the Jews

1933		
	April	The SA organised a boycott of Jewish shops and businesses. They painted 'Jude' (Jew) on windows and tried to persuade the public not to enter. Thousands of Jewish civil servants, lawyers and university teachers were sacked.
	May	A new law excluded Jews from government jobs. Jewish books were burnt.
	September	Jews were banned from inheriting land.

1934	Local councils banned Jews from public spaces such as parks, playing fields and swimming pools.

1935		
	May	Jews were no longer drafted into the army.
	June	Restaurants were closed to Jews all over Germany.
	September	The Nuremberg Laws were a series of measures aimed against the Jews passed on 15 September. This included the Reich Law on Citizenship, which stated that only those of German blood could be German citizens. Jews lost their citizenship, the right to vote and hold government office. The Law for the Protection of German Blood and Honour forbade marriage or sexual relations between Jews and German citizens.

1936		
	April	The professional activities of Jews were banned or restricted – this included vets, dentists, accountants, surveyors, teachers and nurses.
	July–August	There was a deliberate lull in the anti-Jewish campaign as Germany was hosting the Olympics and wanted to give the outside world a good impression.

1937	September	For the first time in two years Hitler publicly attacked the Jews. More and more Jewish businesses were taken over.

1938		
	March	Jews had to register their possessions, making it easier to confiscate them.
	July	Jews had to carry identity cards. Jewish doctors, dentists and lawyers were forbidden to treat Aryans.
	August	Jewish men had to add the name 'Israel' to their first names, Jewish women, the name 'Sarah', to further humiliate them.
	October	Jews had the red letter 'J' stamped on their passports.
	November	*Kristallnacht*. Jewish children were excluded from schools and universities.

ACTIVITIES

1 Make a copy of the table below and give examples of measures which removed Jews' political, social or economic rights. One example has been done for you.

Political	
Economic	
	Boycott of shops
Social	

2 Using a flow diagram, show the key changes in the lives of Jews in Germany 1933–39.

3 How did the position of Jews living in Germany change during the years 1933–39?

Kristallnacht and its aftermath

On 8 November 1938, a young Polish Jew, Herschel Grynszpan, walked into the German Embassy in Paris and shot the first official he met. He was protesting against the treatment of his parents in Germany who had been deported to Poland.

Goebbels used this as an opportunity to organise anti-Jewish demonstrations, which involved attacks on Jewish property, shops, homes and synagogues across Germany. So many windows were smashed in the campaign that the events of 9-10 November became known as *Kristallnacht*, meaning 'Crystal Night' or 'the Night of Broken Glass'. About 100 Jews were killed and 20,000 sent to concentration camps. About 7,500 Jewish businesses were destroyed.

The Nazi government did not permit Jewish property owners to make any insurance claims for damage to property. In addition, any surviving Jewish businesses were not allowed to re-open under Jewish management, but had to have 'pure' Germans in charge of them.

Many Germans were disgusted at *Kristallnacht*. Hitler and Goebbels were anxious that it should not be seen as the work of the Nazis. It was portrayed as a spontaneous act of vengeance by Germans.

> **Source EE:** An account of *Kristallnacht* published in the *Daily Telegraph*, a British newspaper, on 12 November 1938
>
> *Mob law ruled in Berlin throughout the afternoon and evening as hordes of hooligans took part in an orgy of destruction. I have never seen an anti-Jewish outbreak as sickening as this. I saw fashionably dressed women clapping their hands and screaming with glee while respectable mothers held up their babies to see the 'fun'. No attempt was made by the police to stop the rioters.*

> **Source FF:** An account of *Kristallnacht* published in *Der Stürmer*, an anti-Semitic German newspaper, on 10 November 1938
>
> *The death of a loyal party member by the Jewish murderer has aroused spontaneous anti-Jewish demonstrations through the Reich. In many places Jewish shops have been smashed. The synagogues, from which teachings hostile to the state and people are spread, have been set on fire. Well done to those Germans who have ensured revenge for the murder of an innocent German.*

> **Source GG:** A US official describes what he saw in Leipzig
>
> *The shattering of shop windows, looting of stores and dwellings of Jews took place in the early hours of 10 November 1938. In one of the Jewish sections an eighteen-year-old boy was hurled from a three-storey window to land with both legs broken on a street littered with broken beds. The main streets of the city were a positive litter of shattered glass. All the synagogues were gutted by flames.*

Practice question

Study sources EE and FF. Which of the sources is more useful to an historian studying the events of *Kristallnacht*? *(For guidance, see pages 96–97.)*

5 Nazi economic, social and racial policy

▲ **Source HH:** A Jewish shop in Berlin the day after *Kristallnacht*

The aftermath

Hitler officially blamed the Jews themselves for having provoked the attacks and used this as an excuse to step up the campaign against them. He decreed the following:

- The Jews to be fined 1 billion Reichsmarks as compensation for the damage caused.
- Jews can no longer own or manage businesses or shops or employ workers.
- Jewish children can no longer attend Aryan schools.

The persecution continued in 1939:

- In January the Reich Office for Jewish Emigration was established with Reinhard Heydrich as its director. The SS now had the responsibility for removing Jews from Germany completely by forced emigration. They wanted other countries to take the Jews as refugees.
- In the following months Jews were required to surrender precious metals and jewellery.
- On 30 April Jews were evicted from their homes and forced into designated Jewish accommodation or **ghettos**.
- In September, Jews were forced to hand in their radio sets so they could not listen to foreign news.

ACTIVITIES

1 a) How seriously did the following measures threaten the position of Jews in Nazi Germany? Rate them 1–10, with 10 being very serious:
   - ☐ Boycott of Jewish shops 1933
   - ☐ Nuremberg Laws
   - ☐ *Kristallnacht* 1938.
   b) Was *Kristallnacht* the worst problem faced by Jews in Germany in the years 1933–39?

2 Explain why there were changes to the lives of Jewish people in Nazi Germany in the years 1933–39.

Practice question

Did all people living in Germany between 1933 and 1939 welcome the changes introduced by the Nazis? *Use your own knowledge and understanding of the issue to support your answer. (For guidance, see pages 98–99.)*

6 Terror and persuasion

A crucial element in maintaining the Nazi dictatorship was to create a climate of fear – to make people too frightened to oppose actively the Nazi state. This was achieved through the establishment of a police state, including a secret police, the Gestapo, the SS (Schutzstaffel), Nazi control of the legal system and the setting up of concentration camps. Once Hitler had removed opposition, he had to create a state which believed in and supported Nazi ideals. This was achieved through skilful use of propaganda by Goebbels, whose Ministry of Propaganda controlled all aspects of the media, the arts and entertainment.

The use of the SS and the Gestapo

The Nazi police state operated through the use of force and terror. The Nazis used their own organisations to instil fear into the German people. The **SS**, **SD** (*Sicherheitsdienst*, Security Service) and **Gestapo** were the main organisations and in 1936 they were all brought under the control of Heinrich Himmler.

HEINRICH HIMMLER 1900–45

1900	Born near Munich
1918	Joined the army
1923	Joined the Nazi Party and participated in the Munich *Putsch*
1929	Appointed leader of the SS
1930	Elected as a member of parliament
1934	Organised the Night of the Long Knives
1936	Head of all police agencies in Germany
1945	Committed suicide

▼ **Source A:** German citizens searched in the street by the Gestapo and armed uniformed police

The role of the SS (Schutzstaffel)

The SS had been formed in 1925 to act as a bodyguard unit for Hitler and was led by Heinrich Himmler after 1929. Himmler built up the SS until it had established a clear visible identity – members wore black. They showed total obedience to the **Führer**. By 1934 the SS had more than 50,000 members who were to be fine examples of the **Aryan** race and were expected to marry racially pure wives.

After the Night of the Long Knives (see pages 44–45), the SS became responsible for the removal of all opposition to the Nazis within Germany. Membership of the SS and its various bodies had grown to 250,000 by 1939.

The Gestapo

The Gestapo (**Ge**heime **Sta**ats**po**lizei – Secret State Police) was set up in 1933 by Goering (see Source B). In 1936 it came under the control of the SS. It was supervised by Himmler's deputy, a former naval officer, Reinhard Heydrich. By 1939, the Gestapo was the most important police section of the Nazi state. It could arrest and imprison those suspected of opposing the state and its presence was all-pervading (see Source C). The most likely destination for suspects would be a concentration camp run by the SS. It has been estimated that, by 1939, there were about 160,000 people under arrest for political crimes.

> **Source B:** Herman Goering explains about his role in setting up the Gestapo in his book *Germany Reborn*, written in 1934
>
> *Finally, I alone created, on my own initiative, the State Secret Police Department. This is the instrument which is so much feared by the enemies of the State, and which is chiefly responsible for the fact that in Germany and Prussia today there is no question of a Marxist or communist danger.*

> **Source C:** An incident reported in the Rhineland, July 1938
>
> *In a café, a 64-year-old woman remarked to her companion at the table: 'Mussolini [leader of Italy] has more political sense in one of his boots than Hitler has in his brain.' The remark was overheard and five minutes later the woman was arrested by the Gestapo who had been alerted by telephone.*

The *Sicherheitsdienst* (SD)

The *Sicherheitsdienst* (**SD**) was set up in 1931 as the intelligence body of the Nazi Party and was under the command of Heinrich Himmler. Himmler appointed Reinhard Heydrich to organise the department. The main aim of the SD was to discover actual and potential enemies of the Nazi Party and ensure that they were removed.

Members of the SD were employed by the Nazi Party, which paid their salaries. The SD attracted many professional and highly educated people such as lawyers, economists and professors of politics.

> **Interpretation 1:** An extract from *Years of Weimar and the Third Reich* by D. Evans & J. Jenkins
>
> *The SS members were totally dedicated to what they regarded as the supreme virtues of Nazi ideology – loyalty and honour. They saw themselves as the protectors of the Aryan way of life and the defenders of the people against agitators, the criminal classes and those they saw as being responsible for the Jewish–communist threat.*

ACTIVITIES

1. What can you learn from Interpretation 1 about the SS?
2. Study Source B. Why do you think Goering wanted to take credit for the formation of the Gestapo?
3. Use the information in Source C and your own knowledge to explain why the Gestapo was so effective in Nazi Germany.
4. How important were the SS and Gestapo in the Nazi police state?

Practice question

Use Source A and your own knowledge to describe the role of the Gestapo. (For guidance, see pages 91–92.)

Concentration camps

As soon as the Enabling Act had been passed (see page 42), the Nazis established a new kind of prison – a concentration camp – to confine those whom they deemed to be their political, ideological and racial opponents. At first, concentration camps were set up to detain political opponents including communists, socialists, trade unionists, and others who had left-wing and liberal political views. In 1939, there were more than 150,000 people under arrest for political offences.

The SA and SS ran the concentration camps though only the Gestapo had the authority to carry out arrests or interrogations and send people there. The earliest of these was in Dachau, near Munich. Others followed, including Buchenwald, Mauthausen and Sachsenhausen.

Prisoners were classified into different categories and each one was denoted by a different coloured triangle which had to be worn (see Figure 6.1). For example, those who wore black triangles were vagrants and work-shy, pink ones were homosexuals and red ones were political prisoners.

Initially, work in the camps was hard and quite pointless, for example breaking stones, but gradually, the prisoners were used as forced workers in quarries, building, coal mines and armament factories. The camp inmates were underfed and treated with great brutality, and mortality rates were very high. If someone was killed at a concentration camp family members would receive a note saying that the inmate had died of a disease or been shot trying to escape.

Different categories of prisoners

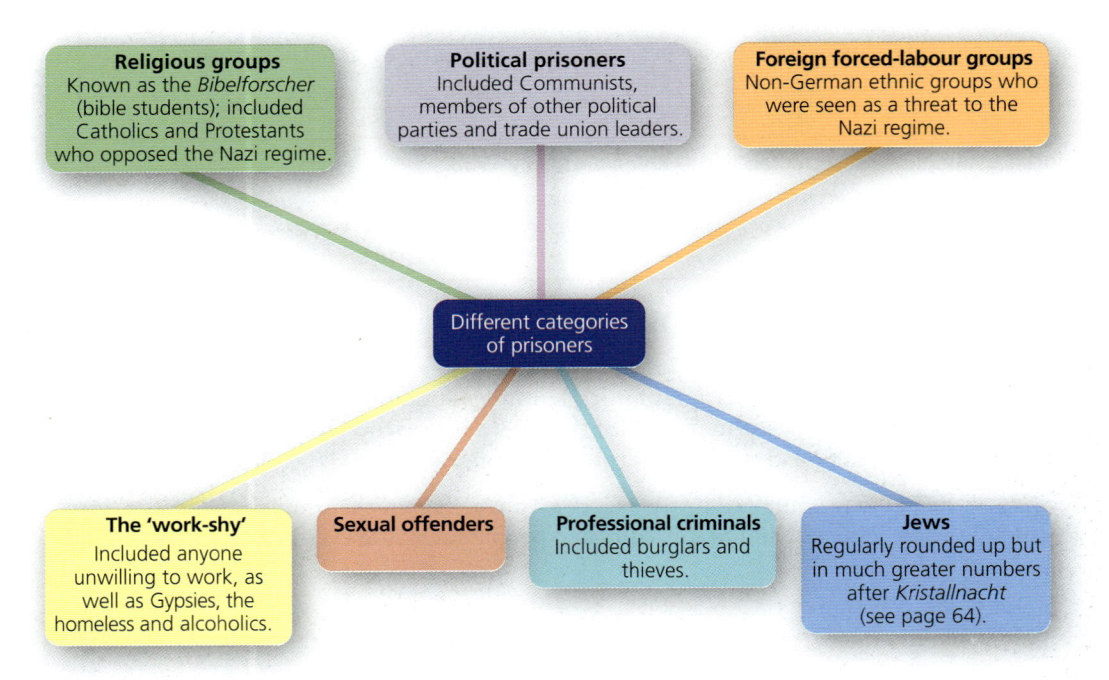

- **Religious groups**: Known as the *Bibelforscher* (bible students); included Catholics and Protestants who opposed the Nazi regime.
- **Political prisoners**: Included Communists, members of other political parties and trade union leaders.
- **Foreign forced-labour groups**: Non-German ethnic groups who were seen as a threat to the Nazi regime.
- **The 'work-shy'**: Included anyone unwilling to work, as well as Gypsies, the homeless and alcoholics.
- **Sexual offenders**
- **Professional criminals**: Included burglars and thieves.
- **Jews**: Regularly rounded up but in much greater numbers after *Kristallnacht* (see page 64).

Figure 6.1: Different categories of prisoner

Practice question

Describe the different categories of prisoner found in a concentration camp. *(For guidance, see page 93.)*

6 Terror and persuasion

◀ Figure 6.2: The position of some of the concentration camps in Germany in the years 1933–39

Interpretation 2: Edward Adler, a survivor, describes his journey to and arrival at Sachsenhausen concentration camp in 1934 (Edward Adler testimony, *Holocaust Encyclopedia*, U.S. Holocaust Memorial Museum)

One particular incident I recall like it was yesterday. An old gentleman with the name of Solomon, I'll never forget. He must have been well into his seventies. He simply couldn't run. He couldn't run and he collapsed, and he lay in the road, and one of the storm troopers stepped on his throat. This is true. Unbelievable, but true, 'til the man was dead. We had to pick up his body and throw him to the side of the road, and we continued on into the camp, where we were assembled in a courtyard, and a strange incident happened at that time. We faced a barrack, a door on the right, a door on the left. People went in the left door, came out the right door, entirely different people. Their hair was shaven off, they had a prisoner's uniform on, a very wide-striped uniform. My number was 6199.

ACTIVITIES

1 Explain the purpose of concentration camps.
2 Study Figure 6.2. What can you learn from the map about the importance of concentration camps in Nazi Germany?

◀ Source D: A photograph showing the arrival of prisoners at Oranienburg, concentration camp in 1933

Practice question

Use Source D and your own knowledge to describe the arrival of prisoners at a concentration camp. *(For guidance, see pages 91–92.)*

69

Control of the legal system

Even though the Nazis controlled the Reichstag and could make laws, Hitler wanted to ensure that all laws were interpreted in a Nazi fashion. The law courts therefore had to experience *Gleichschaltung* (see page 43), just as any other part of society. Some judges were removed, and all the rest had to become members of the National Socialist League for the Maintenance of Law. This meant that Nazi views were upheld in the courts. In October 1933 the German Lawyers Front was established and there were more than 10,000 members by the end of the year. The lawyers had to swear that they would 'strive as German jurists to follow the course of our *Führer* to the end of our days'.

In 1934, a new People's Court was established to try cases of treason. The judges were loyal Nazis. Judges knew that the Minister of Justice would check to see if they had been lenient and sometimes Hitler would alter sentences if he felt that they were too soft. From 1936, judges had to wear the swastika and Nazi eagle on their robes.

Source E: Judge Roland Freisler, State Secretary of the Reich Ministry of Justice, presiding over a People's Court

Practice question

Describe the key features of Nazi control over the legal system. *(For guidance, see page 93.)*

ACTIVITIES

1. Study Source E. What does it show you about Nazi courts?
2. Use Source F and your own knowledge to explain why the Nazis wanted to control the legal system.
3. Study Source G. Can you suggest reasons why the sentence in bold was so crucial to the Nazis?
4. Study Source H. Why do you think this decree was introduced by the Nazis?

Source F: An explanation of the judge's role, put forward by Nazi legal expert Professor Karl Eckhardt in 1936

The judge is to safeguard the order of the racial community, to prosecute all acts harmful to the community and to arbitrate in disagreements. The National Socialist ideology, especially as expressed in the party programme and in the speeches of our Führer, is the basis for interpreting legal sources.

Source G: An extract from the law setting out to change the Penal Code, 28 June 1935

National Socialism considers every attack on the welfare of the national community as wrong. **In future, therefore, wrong may be committed in Germany even in cases where there is no law against what is being done.**

The law-maker cannot give a complete set of rules covering all situations which may occur in life; he therefore entrusts the judge with filling in the remaining gaps.

Source H: Decree for the Protection of the Nationalist Movement against Malicious Attacks upon the Government, 21 March 1933

Whoever purposely makes or circulates a statement of a factual nature which is grossly exaggerated or which may seriously harm the welfare of the Reich is to be punished with imprisonment of up to two years.

Goebbels and propaganda

In March 1934 Josef Goebbels set up the Ministry for Popular Enlightenment and Propaganda to control the thoughts, beliefs and opinions of the German people. It was important for the long-term future of the Third Reich that the majority of the population believed in the ideals of the Nazi Party. Goebbels skilfully used radio, cinema as well as other methods such as rallies to control Germany.

> **Source I:** Goebbels explaining the use of propaganda, in a Nazi magazine
>
> The finest kind of propaganda does not reveal itself. The best propaganda is that which works invisibly, penetrating every cell of life in such a way that the public has no idea of the aims of the propagandist.

ACTIVITY

How useful is Source I to an historian studying the use of propaganda in Nazi Germany?

Radio

All radio stations were placed under Nazi control. Cheap mass-produced radios were sold and could be bought on instalments. By 1939, about 70 per cent of German families owned a radio. Sets were installed in cafés, factories, schools and offices and loudspeakers were placed in streets. It was important that the Nazi message was heard by as many people as possible as often as was possible.

Importantly, the People's Radio lacked shortwave reception, making it difficult for Germans to listen to foreign broadcasts. Hitler and Goebbels regularly made broadcasts.

Cinema

Goebbels also realised the popularity of the cinema. More than 100 films were being made each year and audiences exceeded 250 million in 1933. He was one of the first to appreciate its potential for propaganda. All film plots were shown to Goebbels before going into production. He saw that many Germans were bored by overtly political films. Instead, love stories and thrillers were given pro-Nazi slants. One of the best known was *Hitlerjunge Quex* (1933) which tells the story of a boy who broke away from a communist family to join the **Hitler Youth**, only to be murdered by communists. All film performances were accompanied by a 45-minute official newsreel which glorified Hitler and Germany and publicised Nazi achievements.

One Nazi film director who gained international praise was Leni Riefenstahl. She produced a documentary about the Nazi Party Conference and Rally of 1934 (*Triumph of the Will*) and also one about the 1936 Berlin Olympics.

Hitler ordered Goebbels to make anti-Semitic films; these were not always popular with audiences but were made frequently after 1940.

Rallies

An annual mass rally was held at Nuremberg to advertise the power of the Nazi state and spectacular parades were held on other special occasions such as Hitler's birthday. Local rallies and marches were led by the SA and the Hitler Youth (see page 56). The Nuremberg rallies would last for several days and attracted almost one million people each year after the Nazis came to power.

◀ **Source J:** Workers listening to a broadcast by Hitler

Posters

Posters were cleverly used to put across the Nazi message and many were especially targeted at the young. They were to be seen everywhere and the messages they contained were simple and direct.

▲ **Source K:** A propaganda poster of 1934 which says 'Loyalty, Honour and Order'

Books

All books were carefully censored and controlled to put across the Nazi message. Encouraged by Goebbels, students in Berlin burnt 20,000 books written by Jews, communists and anti-Nazi university professors in a massive bonfire in Berlin in May 1933. There were similar burnings in other cities across Germany that year. Many writers were persuaded or forced to write books which praised Hitler's achievements. Some famous German writers such as Thomas Mann and Bertolt Brecht went into self-imposed exile rather than live under the Nazis. About 2,500 writers left Germany in the years to 1939.

▲ **Source L:** Students and stormtroopers burning books in Berlin in May 1933

Practice question

Describe the methods used by Nazis to control the media in the years 1933–39. *(For guidance, see page 93.)*

ACTIVITIES

1. Study Source L. What does it show you about censorship in Nazi Germany?
2. a) Consider how effective each method of propaganda or censorship would have been (see pages 71–72). Make a copy of the following table and complete it, giving a brief explanation why. One example has been done for you.

	Very effective	Effective	Quite effective	Not effective
Radio	Because it was made available to most homes.			
Cinema				
Posters				
Books				
Rallies				

   b) Which do you think would have had the greatest effect? Why?

Censorship of newspapers and the arts

All aspects of the media including newspapers were censored by Goebbels. The arts were also used by the Nazis as methods of propaganda. Goebbels set up the Reich Chamber of Culture. Musicians, writers and actors had to be members of the Chamber. Any that were thought to be unsuitable were banned. Many left Germany in protest at these conditions.

Newspapers

Non-Nazi newspapers and magazines were closed down. Editors were told what they could print, which meant that the German people only read what the Nazis wanted them to know. Failure by the editors to comply meant arrest and being sent to a concentration camp. By 1935, the Nazis had closed down more than 1,600 newspapers and thousands of magazines. The Reich Press Law was passed in October 1933 and it resulted in the removal of Jewish and left-wing journalists. Editors were told by the Propaganda Ministry what could be printed and any foreign news which was published had to be taken from the Nazi-controlled German Press Agency.

Music

Hitler hated modern music. Jazz, which was 'black' music, was seen as racially inferior and banned. Instead, the Nazis encouraged traditional German folk music together with the classical music of Bach and Beethoven and especially Richard Wagner, who was Hitler's favourite composer.

Theatre

Theatre was to concentrate on German history and political drama. Cheap theatre tickets were made available to encourage people to see plays, which often had a Nazi political or racial theme.

Architecture

Hitler took a particular interest in architecture. He encouraged the 'monumental style' for public buildings. These were large buildings made of stone which were often copies from ancient Greece or Rome and showed the power of the Third Reich. In addition, the 'country style' – traditional buildings with shutters – was used for family homes and hostels to encourage pride in Germany's past. Hitler admired the Greek and Roman style of building because he said the Jews had not 'contaminated' it.

Art

Hitler had earned a living as an artist and believed he was an expert in this area. He hated modern art (any art developed under the Weimar Republic), which he believed was backward, unpatriotic and Jewish. Such art was called 'degenerate' and was banned. In its place, he encouraged art which highlighted Germany's past greatness and the strength and power of the Third Reich. He wanted art to reject the weak and ugly, and to glorify healthy, strong heroes. Artists were therefore expected to portray workers, peasants and women as glorious and noble creatures. After 1934, it was decided that all new public buildings had to have sculptures which demonstrated Nazi ideals. Paintings showed:

- the Nazi ideal of the simple peasant life
- hard work as heroic
- the perfect Aryan – young German men and women were shown to have perfect bodies
- women in their role as housewives and mothers.

▲ **Source M:** The Family. This was painted in 1938 by a Nazi artist, Walter Willrich

ACTIVITIES

1 What message is the artist trying to put across in Source M?
2 You are a visitor to Nazi Germany. Explain how you came across Nazi ideas and views during one day of your stay.

Practice question

Were censorship and propaganda the main methods used by the Nazis to enforce control over the German people between 1933 and 1939? *Use your own knowledge and understanding of the issue to support your answer. (For guidance, see pages 98–99.)*

7 Hitler's foreign policy

Hitler's foreign policy was vital to his rise to power and his maintaining power in Germany. His desire to make Germany a great nation and unite all German-speaking people struck a chord with all sections of German society. From the beginning of his chancellorship in January 1933, his actions made it clear to the major powers that he would present a challenge to the peace settlement of 1919. At all times he presented reasonable grounds for his actions and on occasions he took a gamble such as the re-occupation of the Rhineland in 1936, but his approach seemed to bring success until the crisis over Poland in 1939. The *Anschluss* with Austria in 1938 was accepted but it was the demands for Polish territory and the invasion of that country which precipitated war.

Hitler's foreign policy aims

Much of Hitler's popularity was based on his promise that he would make Germany great again and rid Germany of the hated Treaty of Versailles (see pages 8–9). Hitler had only a few foreign policy aims, most of which revolved around the destruction of the Treaty of Versailles. Hitler outlined his foreign policy aims in his autobiography *Mein Kampf* (see Source A and Figure 7.1 below).

Figure 7.1: Hitler's foreign policy aims ▶

Reverse the Treaty of Versailles
Hitler had never accepted the terms of the Treaty of Versailles and had promised to restore the lands lost in 1919 as well as build up the German armed forces.

Unite all German-speaking people
The Treaty of Versailles had denied Germany national **self-determination**. Hitler wanted to create a 'Greater Germany' (Grossdeutschland) by uniting all Germans into one homeland. For example, there were Germans living in the Sudetenland in Czechoslovakia.

Destroy communism
Hitler was determined to destroy the USSR as he hated **communism**. He believed that communists had helped bring about the defeat of Germany in the First World War. He was also convinced that the Soviet leader, Stalin, wanted to take over Germany.

Anschluss
Hitler supported the *Anschluss* (union) with Austria which had been forbidden by the Treaty of Versailles.

Lebensraum
This was the German word for 'living space'. Greater Germany would have a population of 85 million and would have insufficient lands, food and raw materials. Germany would have to expand in the east to take over Poland and East Russia (see Source A).

Source A: From Hitler's *Mein Kampf*, 1924

We turn our eyes towards the lands of the east … When we speak of new territory in Europe today, we must principally think of Russia and the border states subject to her. Destiny itself seems to wish to point out the way for us here. Colonisation of the eastern frontiers is of extreme importance. It will be the duty of Germany's foreign policy to provide large living spaces for the nourishment and settlement of the growing population of Germany.

ACTIVITIES

1. Study Figure 7.1. What does it tell us about Hitler's foreign policy aims?
2. Why would Hitler's aims be popular with many Germans?

74

Hitler's policies 1933–35

Diplomatically, Hitler was faced with a favourable situation at the beginning of his chancellorship in 1933. The world was just emerging from a huge economic depression and countries were more concerned about focusing on their internal problems than issues abroad.

At this time, the **League of Nations** was seen as weak after its failure to stop Japanese aggression in Manchuria. Importantly, Hitler saw how slow the League was to react to international aggression and how Japan dealt with criticisms from the League. In spite of condemnation by the League of Nations, Japan simply decided to leave the organisation completely. This move showed the powerlessness of the League. Furthermore, Hitler saw that Britain and France, in addition to their economic problems, viewed Italy as the greatest problem for peace and stability in the world since the Fascist leader Benito Mussolini continually spoke of recreating a large empire like the Romans.

Moreover, Hitler knew that in Britain, many people and politicians still felt that Germany had been harshly dealt with by the Treaty of Versailles. Hitler thus realised that if he were to challenge the Treaty of Versailles then there was every chance that he would not face a great deal of opposition.

The Disarmament Conference 1932–34

In 1932, representatives of 60 nations met to discuss ways in which their countries might disarm and so reduce the chance of war. However, the Conference failed to achieve anything – mainly because of differences between France and Germany. Germany insisted that every country should disarm to the lowest level: in other words, reduce their armed forces to match those of Germany (see Source B). When the French, concerned about the growth of German power, refused to co-operate, Hitler withdrew from the Conference. This placed Hitler in a stronger position to rearm on the grounds of equality with other nations.

> **Source B:** From a speech by Hitler to the Reichstag, May 1933
>
> *Germany is at any time willing to undertake further disarmament ... if all other nations are ready ... to do the same. Germany would also be perfectly ready to disband her entire military forces and destroy the small amount of arms remaining to her if the other countries will do the same thing with equal thoroughness.*

During 1933, Hitler announced that the German peacetime army would eventually be 300,000. He would set up a new Air Ministry to train pilots and build 1,000 aircraft. These acts were in direct contravention of the Treaty of Versailles but nothing was done to stop Hitler. He then showed his contempt for the League of Nations in October 1933 by withdrawing Germany's membership.

Non-aggression Pact with Poland, January 1934

By making a Non-aggression Pact with Poland, Hitler showed that he had peaceful intentions in Europe. He promised to accept the borders of Poland (even though some German territory had been given to Poland by the Treaty of Versailles) and he encouraged improved trading between the two countries.

The Pact was set to last ten years and brought Hitler some distinct benefits. It meant he no longer had to fear an attack from Poland (relations had been poor for more than a decade because of ill-feeling over the loss of German land to Poland at the peace settlement). It also created a split between Britain and France because France had a treaty with Poland which covered economic agreements and the aim of following a common foreign policy. It was felt that Hitler had compromised the French treaty. In contrast, Britain saw Hitler's agreement as proof of Hitler's peaceful intentions.

ACTIVITIES

1. Why was the economic depression helpful to Hitler in international relations?
2. You are a British journalist who has visited Nazi Germany in 1933 to investigate Hitler's approach to disarmament. Write an article explaining his policy. Ensure you use Source B in your answer.
3. Explain why the German treaty with Poland was important for Hitler.

Practice question

Study Sources A and B. Which of the sources is more useful to an historian studying Hitler's foreign policy aims? *(For guidance, see pages 96–97.)*

Attempted *Anschluss* with Austria, 1934

In 1934, Hitler suffered a setback in one of his aims: the *Anschluss* (union) with Austria. Hitler had been born in Braunau-am Inn in the former Austro-Hungarian Empire and he saw union with Austria as a natural part of his foreign policy. On coming to power in Germany, he encouraged the large Nazi Party in Austria to agitate for the union with Germany. The Austrian chancellor, Dollfuss, who was determined to maintain Austrian independence, outlawed the Austrian Nazi Party.

However, the Nazi Party in Austria struck back. In July, they attacked the radio station in Vienna and forced the staff to broadcast that Dollfuss had resigned. They then assassinated Dollfuss and tried to seize power. The attempt failed due to a lack of support from Hitler, who was concerned about the possible actions of Benito Mussolini. The Italian dictator regarded himself as the guardian of Austria and he did not favour a strong Germany on the border with Italy. Mussolini moved 100,000 troops to the Austrian frontier to prevent a German takeover. Hitler was forced to deny any involvement in the attempted takeover or the murder of Dollfuss.

Return of the Saarland, January 1935

Following the terms of the Treaty of Versailles, a **plebiscite** was held in the Saarland on 13 January 1935. The Saar, which had been administered by the League of Nations since 1920, voted by 477,000 to 48,000 to rejoin Germany. The plebiscite was administered by the League of Nations and conducted in an open and **democratic** way. On 1 March, the Saar officially became part of Germany once again.

The result was pleasing to Hitler because it showed that there was support for his ideas of bringing all Germans into one nation. It gave him cause for encouragement to follow his other foreign policy aims.

Source C: Citizens of the Saarland, after the result of the plebiscite, January 1935

ACTIVITY

What lessons could Britain and France have learned from Hitler's attempted takeover of Austria in 1934?

Practice question

Use Source C and your own knowledge to describe the results of the Saarland plebiscite. (For guidance, see pages 91–92.)

7 Hitler's foreign policy

Rearmament and conscription

In March 1935 Hitler felt confident enough to announce that he was renouncing the terms of the Treaty of Versailles which dealt with disarmament. **Conscription** was reintroduced and the army, navy and airforce were all built up openly. The *Wehrmacht* (army) was to have about 550,000 men.

Hitler stated that he was building his forces because the two major powers surrounding Germany (France and the Soviet Union) were building up their forces. His actions were therefore determined by self-defence. Rearmament and conscription made Hitler popular within Germany. Jobs were created (see page 48) and people could see that Germany was beginning to be seen as a strong nation once again.

Stresa Front, April 1935

German rearmament alarmed the European powers, and especially France. In a move to restrict German rearmament, France, Italy and Britain met at Stresa, a town in Italy. They formally protested about Hitler's plans to reintroduce conscription and agreed to co-operate among themselves to maintain peace in Europe. This show of unity, known as the Stresa Front, was short-lived due to the:

- Anglo-German Naval Treaty of June 1935 by which Germany was allowed to build a fleet up to 35 per cent of the size of Britain's and the same number of submarines. Britain was accepting Hitler's breach of the Treaty of Versailles and broke the united front established at Stresa. This agreement broke the terms of the Treaty of Versailles and to some observers it seemed as if Britain was condoning German rearmament. It did serve to encourage Hitler to go further in his attempts to reverse the Treaty of Versailles.

- Anglo-French reactions to the Italian invasion of Abyssinia in October 1935 (see textbox). The invasion finally destroyed all co-operation between France, Italy and Britain. Following the Rome–Berlin Axis (see page 80) Mussolini's friendship with Hitler became closer.

The Italian invasion of Abyssinia

In 1935, Italy invaded the African nation of Abyssinia (current-day Ethiopia) in order to expand the Italian empire in east Africa. Mussolini also sought revenge for the defeat in 1896 by Abyssinia at the Battle of Adowa (when Italy had initially tried to conquer Abyssinia). The invasion broke the rules of the League of Nations because Abyssinia was an independent country and a fellow member of the League. Mussolini was condemned for his action and despite attempts by the League, Britain and France to solve the problem, Mussolini's reaction was to leave the League.

ACTIVITIES

1. How useful is Source D to an historian studying Hitler and rearmament?
2. Explain why the Anglo–German Naval Treaty was important for Hitler.
3. Draw up a time line of Hitler's actions from 1933 to 1935. Copy the table and complete each column accordingly.

Date	Event	Result

▼ **Source D:** German army on parade in Berlin, March 1935

Practice question

Describe how Hitler re-armed Germany after 1935. *(For guidance, see page 93.)*

The Rhineland 1936

The Rhineland had been demilitarised under the Treaty of Versailles. The Allies were to occupy the area for fifteen years, or for longer if necessary. Allied troops were withdrawn from the Rhineland in 1935 and in the following March Hitler re-occupied it. On 7 March 1936, Hitler denounced the Locarno Pact (see page 18) and re-occupied the Rhineland. This was a gamble by Hitler, who was convinced that neither Britain nor France, which were both preoccupied with the Abyssinian Crisis (see page 77) would challenge his actions. In fact Hitler had committed virtually his entire trained military forces to the re-occupation and the commanders carried sealed orders, which ordered them to retreat if opposed (see Source E). His gamble succeeded. The re-occupation of the Rhineland convinced Hitler that Britain and France were unlikely to act against further aggression.

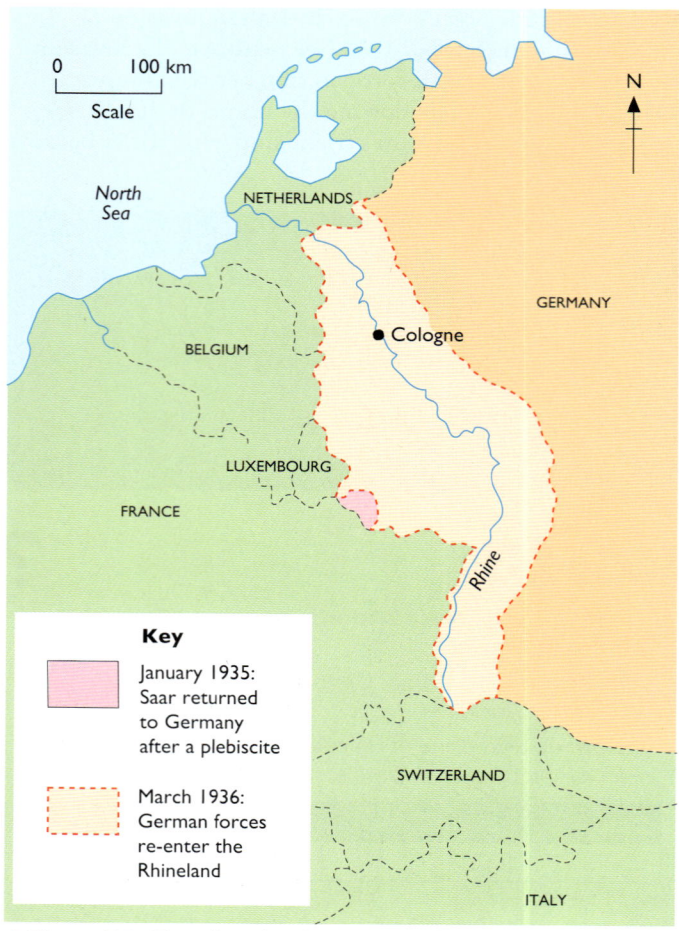

▲ Figure 7.2: The Rhineland

Key
- January 1935: Saar returned to Germany after a plebiscite
- March 1936: German forces re-enter the Rhineland

> **Source E:** From an account written by Hitler's interpreter in 1951
>
> *More than once, during the war, I heard Hitler say: 'The 48 hours after the march into the Rhineland were the most nerve-racking of my life.' He always added: 'If the French had then marched into the Rhineland, we would have had to withdraw with our tails between our legs, for the military resources at our disposal would have been wholly inadequate for even a moderate resistance.'*

▼ **Source F:** German troops entering Cologne in March 1936

Results of the re-occupation of the Rhineland

The success of the Rhineland action improved Hitler's popularity in Germany. A referendum was held asking the German people to approve the re-occupation. Of the 99 per cent of the electorate that voted, 98.8 per cent voted in favour.

Hitler's actions also had important effects on international relations. The threat posed by Germany made it most difficult for Britain and France to deal effectively with the Abyssinian Crisis (see page 77) as they feared that taking firm action against Mussolini would only draw him closer to Hitler. The success of the re-occupation encouraged Hitler to challenge the Treaty of Versailles even more.

◀ **Source G:** A British cartoon about the German re-occupation of the Rhineland. 'Pax Germanica' means 'Peace German-style'

Source H: An entry from *Berlin Diary 1934–41*, by William Shirer, an American journalist living in Berlin in the 1930s, dated 8 March 1936 (Hamish Hamilton, 1941)

Hitler has got away with it. France has done nothing. No wonder the faces of Hitler and Goering were all smiles this noon. Oh the stupidity of the French! I learned today that the German troops who marched into the Rhineland yesterday were under strict orders to beat a hasty retreat if the French army opposed them in any way.

ACTIVITIES

1. Study Source F. This was almost certainly used for propaganda purposes in Germany. Devise a suitable caption for the photograph, from the German point of view.
2. Working in pairs, put together headlines from newspapers in France, Britain, the USA and Germany on the 8 March 1936, reacting to the German re-occupation of the Rhineland.

Practice questions

1. Study Sources E and H. Which of the sources is more useful to an historian studying the German re-occupation of the Rhineland in 1936? (For guidance, see pages 96–97.)
2. What was the purpose of Source G? (For guidance, see pages 94–95.)

Alliances 1936–37

After his successes in 1935 and 1936, Hitler further strengthened the position of Germany by making a series of alliances with Italy and Japan.

The Rome–Berlin Axis

In October 1936, Italy and Germany signed what became known as the Rome-Berlin Axis in which they agreed to work together on matters of mutual interest. Mussolini was keen on closer relations with Germany after Anglo-French opposition to the Italian invasion of Abyssinia. The Axis was an agreement to follow a common foreign policy and central to the agreement was the policy to stop the spread of communism in Europe. The name of the treaty suggested that the affairs of Europe revolved around Italy and Germany. The Axis was strengthened by an interchange of visits by Hitler and Mussolini in 1937 and 1938 (see Source I).

The Anti–Comintern Pact

In November 1936, Hitler signed a treaty with Japan, known as the Anti-Comintern Pact. Comintern refers to the 'Communist International', an organisation set up in Russia in 1919 to support the spread of communism. A year later, in November 1937, Mussolini joined the Pact. The main aim of the Pact was to limit communist influence around the world, more especially that of the Soviet Union. However, it provided scope for much closer relations between Germany, Japan and Italy. The pact encouraged further Japanese expansion into China.

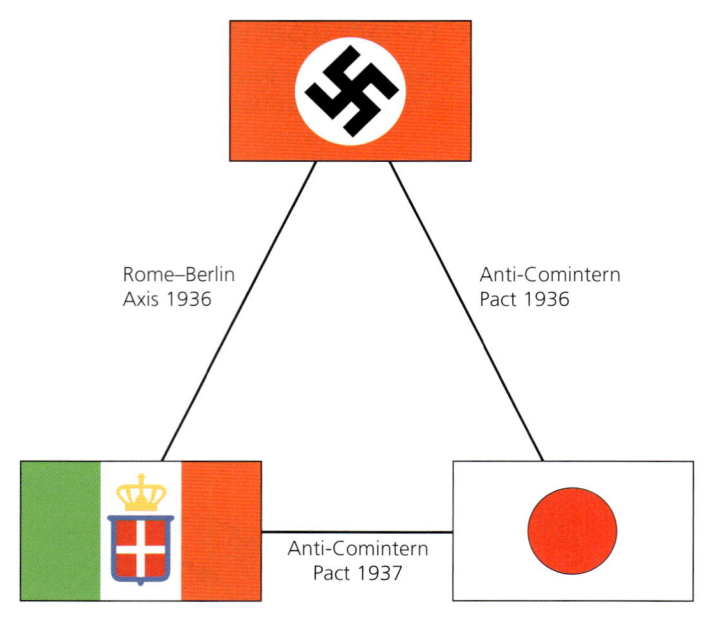

▲ Figure 7.3: Hitler's alliances

ACTIVITY

Explain why the Anti-Comintern Pact was important to Hitler.

Practice question

What was the purpose of Source I? *(For guidance, see pages 94–95.)*

◀ **Source I:** Hitler and Mussolini, during the state visit to Italy, May 1938

Anschluss 1938

After the failure of 1934 (see page 76), in March 1938 Hitler achieved one of his aims, the *Anschluss* with Austria.

Hitler's self-confidence grew considerably after his success in the Rhineland in 1936 (see page 78). On 5 November 1937, he met his military chiefs in Berlin. The meeting lasted three hours and Hitler spoke about his foreign policy ideas for the future. His military **adjutant**, Colonel Hossbach, wrote up the minutes of the meeting five days later from notes and memory. War seemed to be firmly on the agenda. The minutes later became known as the Hossbach Memorandum (see Source J).

> **Source J:** An extract from the Hossbach Memorandum 1937
>
> *The* Führer *stated that the aim of German policy was to make secure and to preserve the racial community and to enlarge it. It was therefore a question of space ... Germany's problem could only be solved by the use of force ... there remained to be answered when and how? ... It was his unalterable decision to solve the problem of living space at the latest by 1943–45.*

Following this meeting, Hitler turned his attention to expansion eastwards.

Hitler was in a much stronger position in 1938:

- He had built up the German armed forces and was encouraged by his success in the Rhineland in 1936 (see page 78) as well as the weaknesses and failures of the League of Nations in Abyssinia (see page 77).
- Mussolini, who had opposed the attempt of 1934, was now an ally of Germany having signed the Rome–Berlin Axis and Anti-Comintern Pact.
- As far as Hitler was concerned, union with Austria was justified under President Wilson's principle of self-determination (at Versailles, President Wilson of the USA had put forward the idea that all people of the same language and culture should exist in the same country). Indeed, 96 per cent of Austrians were German-speaking. Moreover, Hitler himself had been born in Austria.
- The Nazi Party was in a much stronger position in Austria as the new Austrian chancellor, Schuschnigg, had appointed Nazis into his government in return for the promise, which Hitler had no intention of keeping, of respecting the independence of Austria.

> **Source K:** Hitler in conversation with Schuschnigg, March 1938
>
> *Don't think for one moment that anyone on earth is going to thwart my decisions. Italy? I see eye to eye with Mussolini. England? ... And France? France could have stopped Germany in the Rhineland and then we would have had to retreat. But now it is too late for France.*

ACTIVITIES

1. What does Source J suggest about Hitler's aims in Europe?
2. Study Source K. What reasons are suggested for the *Anschluss*?
3. Explain why Hitler decided to carry out the *Anschluss* in 1938.

Events of the Anschluss

The events of the Anschluss can be seen in Figure 7.4.

1936–37	Hitler encouraged the Nazi Party in Austria to stir up trouble for the government. They staged demonstrations demanding union with Germany.
January 1938	Hitler began to step up his campaign by ordering Austrian Nazis to bomb public buildings and stage mass parades.
12 February 1938	Hitler invited the Austrian Chancellor, Schuschnigg, to Germany to discuss the chaos. Schuschnigg was bullied into accepting two Austrian Nazis as members of his cabinet and he also had to accept closer economic ties with Germany.
8 March 1938	On his return to Vienna, Schuschnigg decided to hold a plebiscite to allow the Austrians to vote on the future of their country.
12 March 1938	Hitler, fearing a vote against him, decided to act quickly. He threatened invasion and continued to bully Schuschnigg. Schuschnigg resigned on 12 March 1938 and was replaced by Arthur Seyss-Inquart, leader of the Austrian Nazis. The new leader then asked Hitler to send troops to restore order. German troops marched into Austria.
13 March 1938	The Anschluss was proclaimed.
April 1938	Under the watchful eye of Nazi troops, 99.75 per cent of Austrians voted in favour of the Anschluss.

▲ Figure 7.4: Countdown to the Anschluss

Source L: Hitler addressing a crowd of Austrians in Vienna, 15 March 1938

1 Immigration

During the late nineteenth and early twentieth centuries about 40 million people emigrated to the USA. The majority of these came from Southern and Eastern Europe and became known as the 'new immigrants'. This distinguished them from the 'old immigrants' who had arrived from Western and Northern Europe in the earlier part of the nineteenth century. However, by the early 1920s, there was not only open hostility towards immigrants but also a growing xenophobia (fear of foreigners) in the USA. Many immigrants from Eastern Europe were thought to be communists or anarchists (people who do not respect authority) and this resulted in the growth of the Red Scare. A consequence of this fear of communism was the Palmer Raids and the trial of two Italian immigrants, Sacco and Vanzetti, who became scapegoats for the xenophobia that emerged during the 1920s.

The Open Door policy and reasons for emigration to the USA

People made the journey to the USA for many different reasons. These can be grouped into the 'push' and 'pull' factors. The push factors explain why immigrants wanted to leave their homeland and the pull factors relate to the attractions of a new life in the USA. Land was available for farming, though by 1900, good cheap agricultural land was becoming scarce. The USA was booming industrially, there were many employment opportunities and those with any business acumen could start new ventures quite easily. The USA was the land of opportunity for all. It was seen as the land of the free and a country which guaranteed basic human rights. For example, Jews from Eastern Europe were seeking religious freedom and an escape from the **pogroms** of Russia, where many thousands had been massacred. In short, the homelands of the immigrants offered none of these attractions. Moreover, the US government followed an **'Open Door' policy**. During the late nineteenth century, mass migration was encouraged by the US government which was keen to populate the continent. The Open Door policy was designed to make entry into the country as easy as possible.

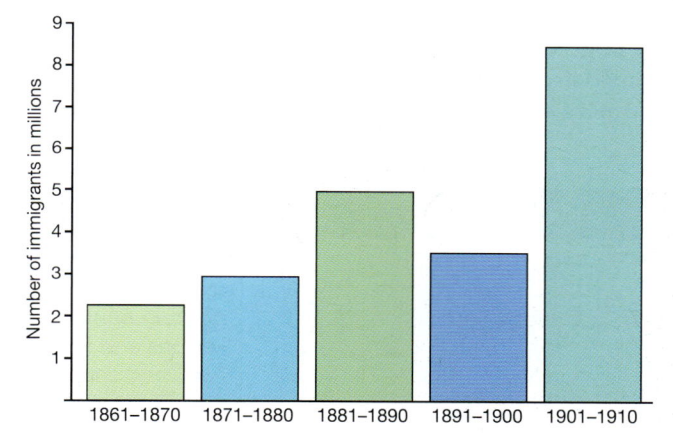

▲ **Source A:** Official government statistics showing the number of immigrants arriving in the USA, 1871–1920

ACTIVITIES

1. Study Interpretation 1. What were the push and pull factors that attracted immigrants to America in the early twentieth century?
2. Working in pairs, devise a suitable poster or advertisement to attract people to the USA in the early twentieth century.

Interpretation 1: From the autobiography of Louis Adamic who emigrated to the USA from Slovenia in 1913. His book *From Laughing in the Jungle* was published in 1932

My notion of the United States is that it was a grand, amazing, somewhat fantastic place – the Golden Country – huge beyond conception, very exciting. In America one could make pots of money in a short time, acquire immense holdings, wear a white collar and have polish on one's boots – and eat white bread, soup and meat on weekdays as well as on Sundays, even if you were only an ordinary workman. In America even the common people were 'citizens' and not 'subjects' as in many European countries.

Practice question

Use Source A and your own knowledge to describe immigration into the USA between 1870 and 1910. *(For guidance, see pages 159–160)*

Opposition to immigration and demands for restriction

By 1910 there were many in the USA who began to oppose the mass immigration. The immigrants moved to cities where they tended to live with people from their own country of origin and hence **ghettos** developed. Intolerance began to grow and there was a feeling that the 'new' immigrants would take jobs and work for very low wages. It was also thought that the immigrants were responsible for increases in crime, drunkenness and prostitution (see Source B).

There was opposition to further immigration when the USA became involved in the First World War and hostility to German immigrants increased alarmingly. Indeed, the teaching of German was banned in schools in several states. Furthermore, involvement in the First World War caused many Americans to fear future entanglements in European affairs. They wanted the USA to isolate itself from events in Europe and restricting immigration was a way of doing this.

In the larger cities, the more established immigrant groups such as Irish and German Americans tended to look down on the more recent immigrants from Eastern Europe and Italy. For many Americans in the 1920s, the ideal citizen was a **WASP** – white, Anglo-Saxon and Protestant. Asian immigrants were not white while many recent European immigrants were Catholics, Greek Orthodox or Jewish. Above all, many Americans feared that immigrants would bring with them dangerous political beliefs, especially **communism**.

Government legislation

Immigration was restricted by a series of measures, as detailed in Table 1.1. In addition to the restrictions on the numbers of immigrants (see Sources D and E), measures were introduced to Americanise them (see Source C). The Federal Bureau of Naturalization organised naturalisation proceedings and patriotic 'Americanization Day' rallies. The Americanization Day was designed for citizens to re-affirm their loyalty to the USA and the heritage of freedom. People were invited to put on appropriate ceremonies in schools and similar places. Courses on politics and democracy were organised by the Federal Bureau of Education to prepare immigrants for the citizenship examination.

Date	Measure	Key features
1917	Literacy Test	All foreigners wishing to enter the USA had to take a literacy test. They had to prove that they could read a short passage in English. Many people from poorer countries, especially in Eastern Europe, could not afford to take English lessons and failed the test. In addition, the act banned all immigration from Asia, and charged an immigration fee of $8.
1921	Emergency Quota Act	This act introduced a quota system. New immigrants were allowed in as a proportion of the number of people of the same nationality who had been living in the USA in 1910. The figure was set at three per cent. In other words, the Act reduced the numbers of immigrants from Eastern Europe.
1924	National Origins Act	The quota was reduced to two per cent of the 1890 census. In other words, since there had been a lot more people arriving from Northern Europe by 1890, more of these groups were allowed to enter. (See Source D on page 103.)
1929	Immigration Act	This restricted immigration to 150,000 per year. There were to be no Asians at all. Northern and Western Europeans were allocated 85 per cent of places. By 1930, immigration from Japan, China and Eastern Europe had virtually ceased.

▲ Table 1.1: Measures to reduce immigration 1917–29

1 Immigration

Source B: From a speech by a senator from Alabama in 1921 who was in favour of the laws to restrict immigration

The steamship companies haul them over to America, and as soon as they step off the decks of their ships the problem of the steamship companies is settled, but our problem has begun – Bolshevism, red anarchy, black-handers, kidnappers, challenging the authority and integrity of the flag. Thousands come here who never take the oath to our Constitution and to become citizens of the USA. They pay allegiance to our country while they live upon the substance of their own. They fill places that belong to the loyal wage-earning citizens of America. They are of no service whatever to our people. They are a menace and a danger to us every day.

Source C: President Calvin Coolidge, a **Republican**, speaking to Congress in 1923

We must remember that every object of our institutions of society and government will fail unless America is kept American. New arrivals should be limited to our capacity to absorb them into the ranks of good citizenship. America must be kept American. I am convinced that our present economic and social conditions warrant a limitation of those to be admitted. Those who do not want to be partakers of the American spirit ought not to settle in America.

Country	Quota
Germany	51,227
Great Britain and Northern Ireland	34,007
Sweden	9,561
Norway	6,453
Italy	3,845
Czechoslovakia	3,073
Russia	2,248
Romania	603

▲ **Source D:** Annual immigration quotas (in thousands) for some countries under the 1924 National Origins Act

▲ **Source E:** An American cartoon of 1921 commenting on the immigrant quotas

ACTIVITIES

1. What was meant by Americanisation?
2. Explain why there was a growth in opposition to immigration into the USA.
3. What do Sources D and E suggest about the attempts to restrict immigration in the early 1920s?
4. How successful had the US government been in its attempts to restrict immigration by 1929?

Practice questions

1. Describe how restrictions were placed on immigration into the USA after 1917. *(For guidance, see page 161.)*
2. Study Sources B and C. Which of the sources is more useful to an historian studying the reasons for restricting entry to immigrants? *(For guidance, see pages 164–165.)*

103

The growth of xenophobia

As more and more immigrants entered the country, especially from the countries of Eastern Europe which had experienced political changes resulting from the First World War, there was a corresponding growth of xenophobia within America. This displayed itself in a number of ways:

The 'Red Scare'

The 'Red Scare' was an almost hysterical reaction from many US citizens to developments in Europe in the years 1917–19, especially the fear of communism. In Russia in 1917, the Bolshevik Revolution led to the establishment of a communist government. In Germany, a group of communists attempted to seize power in January 1919.

Many Americans were convinced that revolutionary ideas were being brought to the USA by immigrants, especially from Eastern Europe. Moreover, Americans tended to see any new political ideas, especially radicalism and anarchism, as branches of communism (see Source G). All people who believed in these ideas were classified as 'Reds' (communists). When a communist party was formed in the USA in 1919, many Americans began to fear that there would be a revolution in their own country.

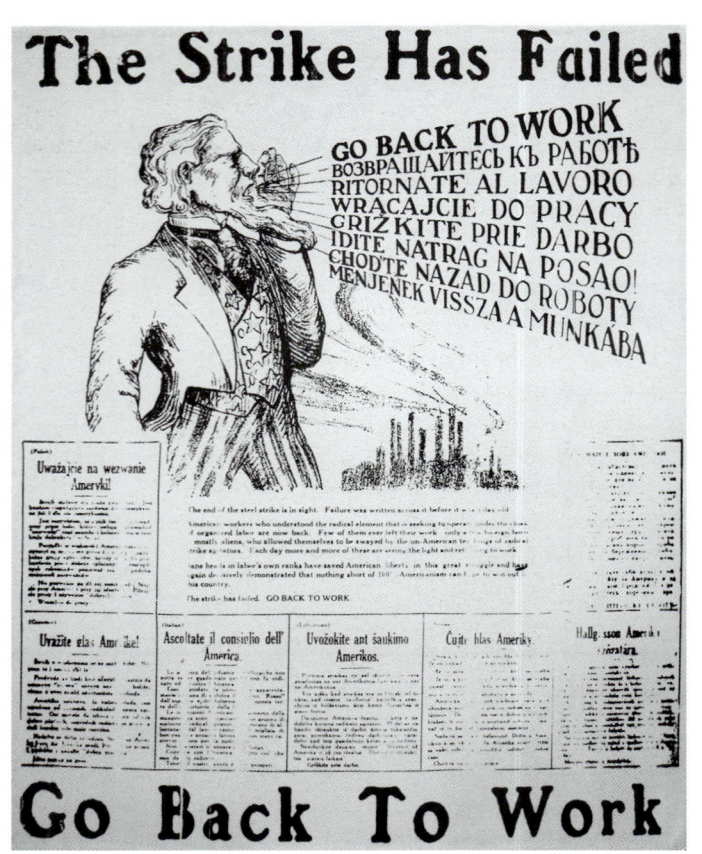

Strikes

There were 3,600 strikes in 1919. They were protests against poor working conditions and low pay. Even the police went on strike in Boston. To many members of the American public, the strikes seemed to herald the beginnings of a communist revolution.

A general strike in Seattle was led by an organisation known as the Industrial Workers of the World (IWW), a name that many found strongly suggestive of communist ideals. The strike failed and one consequence was the loss of orders for the dockyards, which resulted in an increase in unemployment.

During the steelworkers' dispute, the steel company owners published circulars which attacked foreign-born strikers. The press generally portrayed the strikes as anti-American actions which threatened the US government.

▲ **Source F:** An advertisement in a US newspaper encouraging steelworkers to return to work, 1919. It was written in eight languages, which linked union leadership with foreigners and the un-American teachings of radical strike agitators

> **Source G:** From 'The case against the Reds', an essay by Attorney General Mitchell Palmer, 1920
>
> It is my belief that while they have stirred discontent in our midst, while they have caused irritating strikes, and while they have infected our social ideas with the disease of their own minds and their unclean morals we can get rid of them and not until we have done so shall we have removed the menace of Bolshevism for good.

Events connected with anarchists

In 1919, there was a series of bombings by extreme anarchist groups. Anarchists were anti-government in their views and did not respect the rules of law and order. Their aim was to disrupt and ultimately destroy the functions of government. In one famous attack, the home of Mitchell Palmer, the Attorney-General (Head of the US Department of Justice), was bombed. In April 1919, a bomb planted in a church in Milwaukee killed ten people. In May, letter bombs were posted to 36 well-known Americans.

> **Source H:** An anarchist pamphlet called the *Plain Truth*, found near the house of Mitchell Palmer in 1919
>
> There will have to be bloodshed. We will not dodge. There will have to be a murder. We will kill. There will have to be destruction. We will destroy. We are ready to do anything to suppress the capitalist system.

Practice questions

1. What was the purpose of Source F? *(For guidance, see pages 162–163.)*
2. Use Source I and your own knowledge to describe the Palmer Raids. *(For guidance, see pages 159–160.)*

The Palmer Raids

The press whipped up public feeling and insisted that the attack on the home of Mitchell Palmer was further evidence of a widespread communist takeover plot. The police attacked **socialist** parades on May Day 1920 and raided the offices of socialist organisations. Many innocent people were arrested because of their supposed dangerous political beliefs. Amongst those arrested were **trade unionists**, black people, Jews and Catholics. These arrests were known as the 'Palmer Raids' as they were organised by Mitchell Palmer. These raids were illegal but there were few who protested against them. In all, more than 6,000 suspected communists were arrested in 36 cities across the USA. Several hundred Russian immigrants were sent back in a ship nicknamed the 'Soviet Ark'.

ACTIVITIES

1. What do the following terms mean: rugged individualism, communism, anarchism and radical?
2. Explain why there was a fear of revolution in the USA in 1919.
3. What do Sources G and H tell us about the fear of revolution in the USA by 1920?

▲ **Source I:** The aftermath of one of the Palmer Raids on the offices of the Industrial Workers of the World (IWW), 15 November 1919

The Sacco and Vanzetti case

On 5 May 1920, two Italian labourers, Nicola Sacco and Bartolomeo Vanzetti, were arrested and charged with the murder of Fred Parmenter. Parmenter was the paymaster of a factory in South Braintree, Massachusetts. Parmenter and a security guard had been shot by two armed robbers on 15 April 1920. Both men died, but not before Parmenter had described his attackers as slim foreigners with olive skins.

The Sacco and Vanzetti trial began in May 1921 and lasted 45 days. Owing to the heavy publicity given to the case, it took several days to find a jury of 12 men who were acceptable to both the prosecution and defence. In all, 875 candidates were called to the court. On 14 July 1921, the jury delivered a guilty verdict. There were demonstrations all over the USA in support of the two condemned men (see Source L). Sacco and Vanzetti took their case to appeal in several higher courts but all attempts failed. The last appeal was in 1927. The two men were executed by electric chair on 24 August 1927.

THE EVIDENCE AGAINST SACCO AND VANZETTI

- They were anarchists who hated American **capitalism** and the American system of government.
- Vanzetti had been convicted of armed robbery in 1919.
- Sixty-one eyewitnesses identified the two men as the killers.
- Sacco and Vanzetti were carrying guns on the day they were arrested.
- The two men told lies in their statements to the police.
- Forensic evidence matched the pistol that killed the guard with the one carried by Sacco.
- Vanzetti refused to take the stand at the trial.

▲ Figure 1.1: Bartolomeo Vanzetti (left) and Nicola Sacco (right)

THE EVIDENCE IN THEIR DEFENCE

- Vanzetti refused to take the stand because he feared that his political activities would become a major focus and that he would be found guilty of these rather than the robbery.
- One hundred and seven people confirmed the two men's alibi (their claim that they were somewhere else when the robbery was committed). However, many of these witnesses were recently arrived Italian immigrants whose English was poor.
- Some believe that the forensic evidence about Sacco's gun was rigged.
- Evidence from the 61 prosecution witnesses often disagreed in important details. Some witnesses had changed their stories by the time the trial started.
- The two men said they lied to the police because they feared that they would be discriminated against because of their support for anarchism.
- Several other men confessed to the crime.
- The judge, Webster Thayer, seemed determined to find the two men guilty.

1 Immigration

Importance of the trial

- The trial was reported all over the world and showed the intolerance of American society. As Italian immigrants, the two men were victims of racial discrimination and were denied rights that they were entitled to.
- It exposed the unfairness of the American legal system. The two men were convicted on flimsy evidence, although subsequent evidence suggests that Sacco may have been guilty.
- In the 1970s the **Governor** of Massachusetts granted Sacco and Vanzetti a formal pardon and agreed that a mistrial had taken place.

Source J: Freda Kirchwey was in Germany during the last few weeks before Nicola Sacco and Bartolomeo Vanzetti were executed. She wrote about her reaction to the execution in *The Nation*, 28 August 1927. *The Nation* was a radical American magazine

We've hardly talked about it – but every time we got within range of a newspaper we've rushed to it hoping, without any real hope, that some miracle of mercy would have descended on the Governor or someone else. It was hard to sleep through some of those nights. And everywhere we went – from Paris and Berlin to Heiligenblut in the Austrian Tyrol – people talked to us about it with horror and a complete inability to understand. It whipped up further opposition to immigrants, intensified the 'Red Scare' and seemed to strengthen the case for restrictions on immigration.

Source K: A comment made about Judge Thayer who presided over the original Sacco and Vanzetti case. It was made in 1930 by Felix Frankfurter, a lawyer who campaigned for a retrial, and who wrote a book which criticised the original trial

I have known Judge Thayer all my life. I say that he is a narrow-minded man; he is an unintelligent man; he is full of prejudice; he is carried away by fear of Reds, a fear which has captured about ninety per cent of the American people.

ACTIVITIES

1 Examine the evidence for and against the two men on pages 106–107. Copy and complete the table below. Now make your own decision: guilty or not guilty? Write two paragraphs explaining your decision.

	Guilty	Not guilty
Most convincing evidence		
Least convincing evidence		

2 What is the main message of Source L?

Practice questions

1. Study Sources J and K. Which of the sources is more useful to an historian studying the Sacco and Vanzetti case? *(For guidance, see pages 164–165).*
2. Was the fear of Communism the most important reason for the restrictions on immigration into the USA in the 1920s? Use your own knowledge and understanding of the issue to support your answer. *(For guidance, see pages 166–167)*

◀ **Source L:** Demonstrators in Boston in 1925 in support of Sacco and Vanzetti

2 Religion and race

The period 1910 to 1929 witnessed the growth and development of religious fundamentalism, particularly in the Bible Belt region of south-east America. The Monkey Trial highlighted the gulf between many American citizens. Some Americans suffered due to racism and bigotry, particularly Native Americans and African Americans. During the 1920s there was a great deal of hatred towards black Americans who were forced to live according to the restrictions of segregation and the Jim Crow laws. It was a period which witnessed the growth of racial intolerance and the growth of the Ku Klux Klan. While some black Americans migrated north in the hope of avoiding persecution, others attempted to fight back through the work of organisations such as the NAACP and the UNIA.

Religious fundamentalism and the Bible Belt

In the 1920s, most rural Americans were very religious people. The south-east of the USA (including states such as Alabama, Arkansas, Kentucky and Tennessee) had been given the name of the '**Bible Belt**' and the people viewed themselves as righteous, God-fearing Christians (see Figure 2.1). Many in these areas were known as **Fundamentalists** following the formation of the World's Christian Fundamentals Association. They were Protestants who believed that everything in the Bible was to be taken literally and must not be questioned.

During the 1920s, many people in the Bible Belt sought to hold back the changes that were taking place in the USA. They disliked what they saw as provocative clothes and dancing, the gambling and what they saw as the general decline in moral standards. One of the most famous Fundamentalist preachers was Aimee Semple McPherson. She went round the USA in the early 1920s raising money for her Four Square Gospel Church. She raised more than $1.5 million in 1921 for the building of her Angelus Temple.

The gap in belief between the rural and urban Americans was most clearly seen with the argument over the theory of evolution. Most people living in the towns and cities of the USA accepted Charles Darwin's theory of evolution, which stated that over a period of millions of years human beings had evolved from ape-like creatures. However, these views were not accepted by many people in rural areas, especially in the Bible Belt states (see Source A).

> **Source A:** A sermon delivered by Billy Sunday, a well-known Fundamentalist preacher in 1925
>
> If anyone wants to teach that God-forsaken hell-born, bastard theory of evolution, then let him ... but do not expect the Christian people of this country to pay for the teaching of a rotten, stinking professor who gets up there and teaches our children to forsake God and makes our schools a clearing-house for their God-forsaken dirty politics.

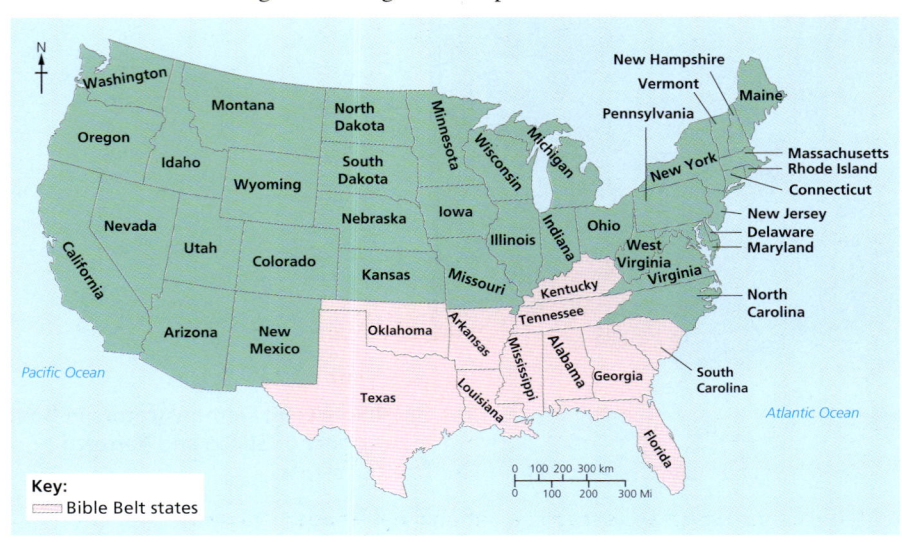

◀ Figure 2.1: The Bible Belt

The Monkey Trial

In 1924, the state of Tennessee passed the Butler Act, which made it illegal for any public school 'to teach any theory which denied the story of the Divine Creation of man as taught in the Bible and to teach that man has descended from a lower order or animals'. Five other states passed similar laws.

A biology teacher called John Scopes decided to challenge this ban. He deliberately taught evolution in his class in Tennessee in order to be arrested and put on trial. Both sides hired the best lawyers for a trial, which took place in July 1925. Its proceedings captured the imagination of the public. Scopes was supported by the American Civil Liberties Union and defended by Clarence Darrow, a famous criminal lawyer, and the prosecutor was William Jennings Bryan, a Fundamentalist. Scopes was convicted of breaking the law and was fined $100. However, the trial was a disaster for the public image of the Fundamentalists. The trial became a debate between science and religion. Bryan was shown to be confused and ignorant while the media mocked the beliefs of those who opposed the theory of evolution. Many saw the Fundamentalist viewpoint as an attempt to stifle freedom of thought.

> **Source B:** A report on the trial in the *Baltimore Evening Sun*, July 1925
>
> For nearly two hours Mr Darrow goaded his opponent. He asked Mr Bryan if he really believed that the serpent had always crawled on its belly because it tempted Eve, and if he believed Eve was made from Adam's rib. Bryan's face flushed under Mr Darrow's searching words and when one stumped him he took refuge in his faith and either refused to answer directly or said in effect: 'The Bible states it; it must be true'.

ACTIVITIES

1. Explain why John Scopes was put on trial in 1925.
2. Does Source C support the views of the evolutionists or the anti-evolutionists? Give reasons to support your answer.

Practice question

Study Sources A and B. Which of the sources is more useful to an historian studying the Monkey Trial?
(For guidance, see pages 164–165.)

CLASSROOM IN PROPOSED BRYAN UNIVERSITY OF TENNESSEE

▲ **Source C:** A cartoon which appeared in a national newspaper in July 1925

ACTIVITIES

1. Explain why the US government wanted to 'Americanise' the Native Americans.
2. Study Source D. What does it tell you about the lives of Native Americans during the period 1910–29?

Practice question

Describe how Native Americans were treated by the US government during the 1920s. *(For guidance, see page 161.)*

The treatment of Native Americans

At the beginning of the twentieth century, Native Americans had been placed on reservations. In 1924 the Indian Citizenship Act was passed. This at last granted full American citizenship to America's native peoples (they were called 'Indians' in the Act).

Native Americans were really only seen when they were demonstrating Indian crafts, speaking Indian languages, or performing in stereotypical Indian costume. In the states of Vermont and New Hampshire, the Eugenics Project had a programme which managed Native Americans and other 'undesirables' by means of social planning, education, and reproductive control. Some white reformers argued that Native Americans could only survive by rejecting their own culture and merging fully into white society. As a result, special boarding schools were established for this purpose and thousands of Native American children were taken from their families and cultures. This tended to destroy the identity of tribes and the children were encouraged not to speak their own language and convert to Christianity. It was another attempt to Americanise those people who were not the original migrants in the USA (see pages 101-103).

In 1928, the Meriam Report was prepared for the American government. The report stated that the boarding schools were underfunded and understaffed and run too harshly. The attempt to bring assimilation by means of education had failed. The Report recommended that the curriculum, which taught only European-American cultural values, should be dropped. The report went on to say that the Native Americans should be provided with the skills and education for life in their own traditional rural communities as well as American urban society.

▲ **Source D:** A Native American logger and his family outside their home in Washington State, 1916

Segregation and the Jim Crow laws

Black people had been brought to America as slaves in the seventeenth and eighteenth centuries. By the time slavery was ended in the 1860s, there were more black Americans than whites living in the southern states. White-controlled state governments, fearing the power of black Americans, introduced laws to control their freedom. These were known as the Jim Crow laws, after a nineteenth-century comedian's act that ridiculed black people. They segregated blacks in schools, parks, hospitals, swimming pools, libraries and other public places. New Jim Crow laws were passed in some states so that there were segregated taxis, race tracks and boxing matches.

Blacks found it hard to get fair treatment. They could not vote and were denied access to good jobs and a reasonable education. They were intimidated by whites who tried to control them through fear and terror. In the First World War, 360,000 black Americans served in the armed forces. They returned home to find that racism was part of everyday life. Between 1915 and 1922 more than 430 black Americans were lynched.

ACTIVITY

Explain why segregation was introduced into the southern states.

Practice question

Use Source E and your own knowledge to describe the main features of segregation. (For guidance, see pages 159–160.)

◀ Source E: A segregated drinking fountain

◀ Source F: Jesse Washington, an 18-year-old black African American, lynched May 1916 at Waco, Texas

The Ku Klux Klan (KKK)

Origins

The Ku Klux Klan (KKK) was set up in the 1860s by soldiers who had fought in the American Civil War. Its aim was to terrorise black people newly freed from slavery. However, it died out in the years after 1870 when a federal Grand Jury determined that the Klan was a 'terrorist organisation'. It was revived after the release of a film, *The Birth of a Nation*, in 1915, which was set in the south after the Civil War and depicted the Klan saving white families from gangs of black people intent on raping and looting. The film attracted huge audiences and aimed to reinforce the idea of **white supremacy**.

After the First World War, labour tensions rose as veterans tried to enter the workforce. In reaction to new groups of immigrants and migrants (see pages 101–103), the membership increased.

Beliefs

The Klan members were WASPs. They identified themselves as white, Anglo-Saxon, Protestants, and they saw themselves as being superior to other races. They were also anti-communist, anti-black, anti-Jew, anti-Catholic and against all foreigners.

Organisation

Klansmen dressed in white robes and wore white hoods. This outfit was designed to conceal the identity of Klan members, who often attacked their victims at night. The white colour symbolised white supremacy. Members carried American flags and lit burning crosses at their night-time meetings. Their leader, a dentist called Hiram Wesley Evans, was known as the Imperial Wizard (see Source G). Officers of the Klan were known as Klaliffs, Kluds or Klabees.

> **Source G:** Hiram Wesley Evans, the leader of the KKK, speaking in 1924
>
> It is the way of the world that each race must fight for its life, must conquer or accept slavery or die. The Klan wants every state to make sex between a white and black person a crime. Protestants must be supreme. Rome shall not rule America. The Roman Catholic Church is un-American and usually anti-American.

▼ **Source H:** Members of the Ku Klux Klan marching through Washington DC, 18 August 1925

Membership

In 1920 the Klan had 100,000 members. By 1925, it claimed to have more than 5 million. It attracted members all over the USA, but especially in the south. The state governors of Oregon and Oklahoma were members of the Klan. The growth of the Klan after 1920 arose in response to:

- Industrialisation, which brought more and more workers to cities. The Klan grew rapidly in cities such as Memphis and Atlanta, which expanded quickly after 1910.
- Many of these workers were immigrants from Eastern and Southern Europe, or black Americans migrating from the southern states to the urban centres of the north.
- Southern whites resented the arming of black soldiers during the First World War.

Activities

Members of the Klan carried out lynchings of black people and they beat up and mutilated anyone they considered to be their enemy (see Sources I and J). They stripped some of their victims and put tar and feathers on their bodies. For example:

- In 1921 Chris Lochan, a restaurant owner, was run out of town because he was accused of being a foreigner. His parents were Greek.
- George Arnwood was a mentally retarded black man who, in October 1933, was accused of assaulting an 82-year-old white woman. Members of the Klan dragged him from jail and beat him to death. His body was strung up on a tree and then dragged through the town before being set on fire. The police watched and did nothing.

Decline

The Klan declined after 1925 when one of its leaders, Grand Wizard David Stephenson, was convicted of the rape and mutilation of a woman on a Chicago train. The scandal destroyed Stephenson's reputation and when the Governor of Indiana refused to pardon him, he produced evidence of illegal Klan activities. This discredited the Klan and led to a sharp decline in its membership.

> **Source I:** A description of Klan activities in Alabama in 1929 from *Current History* written by R.A.Patton
>
> A lad whipped with branches until his back was ribboned flesh ... a white girl, divorcee, beaten into unconsciousness in her home; a naturalised foreigner flogged until his back was a pulp because he married an American woman; a negro lashed until he sold his land to a white man for a fraction of its value.

> **Source J:** A report of KKK activities by the New York magazine *World* in 1921
> - 5 kidnappings
> - 43 orders to Negroes to leave town
> - 27 tar and featherings
> - 41 floggings
> - 1 branding with acid
> - 1 mutilation
> - 4 murders

ACTIVITIES

1. What does Source G suggest about the beliefs of the Ku Klux Klan?
2. Compile an entry for a webpage detailing the activities of the KKK during the 1920s.
3. Using Sources H (page 112), I and J, design a poster for those people who opposed the activities of the KKK. The poster should aim to shock people.

Practice question

Use Source H and your own knowledge to describe the key features of the KKK organisation. *(For guidance, see pages 159–160.)*

Why was no action taken against the Ku Klux Klan?

Some states believed that the **federal government** had no right to interfere in what was happening with the Klan. In addition, many politicians in the south knew that if they spoke out against the Klan, they would lose votes and might not be elected to **Congress**. When campaigning for re-election in 1924, one Congressman said 'I was told to join the Klan or else.'

> **Interpretation 1:** From *Konklave in Kokomo*, a book about the Ku Klux Klan by the historian Robert Coughlan (1949). Coughlan grew up in Kokomo during the 1920s
>
> Literally half the town (Kokomo) belonged to the Klan when I was a boy. At its peak, which was from 1923 through 1925, the Nathan Hale Den had about five thousand members, out of an able-bodied adult population of ten thousand. With this strength the Klan was able to dominate local politics. It packed the police and fire departments with its own people, with the result that on parade nights the traffic patrolmen disappeared and traffic control was taken over by sheeted figures whose size and shape resembled those of the vanished patrolmen.

> **Interpretation 2:** A historian writing about the Ku Klux Klan in 1992
>
> The Ku Klux Klan believed White, Protestant America had to be saved from black people, immigrants, Jews and Catholics. They used extreme violence against people from all these groups, especially black people. Klan members swore an oath of loyalty to the USA and promised to defend the USA against 'any cause, government, people, sect or ruler that is foreign to the country'.

ACTIVITY

Study Source K and Interpretation 1. Explain why the Ku Klux Klan was able to operate freely in the 1920s.

Practice question

What was the purpose of Source K? *(For guidance, see pages 162–163.)*

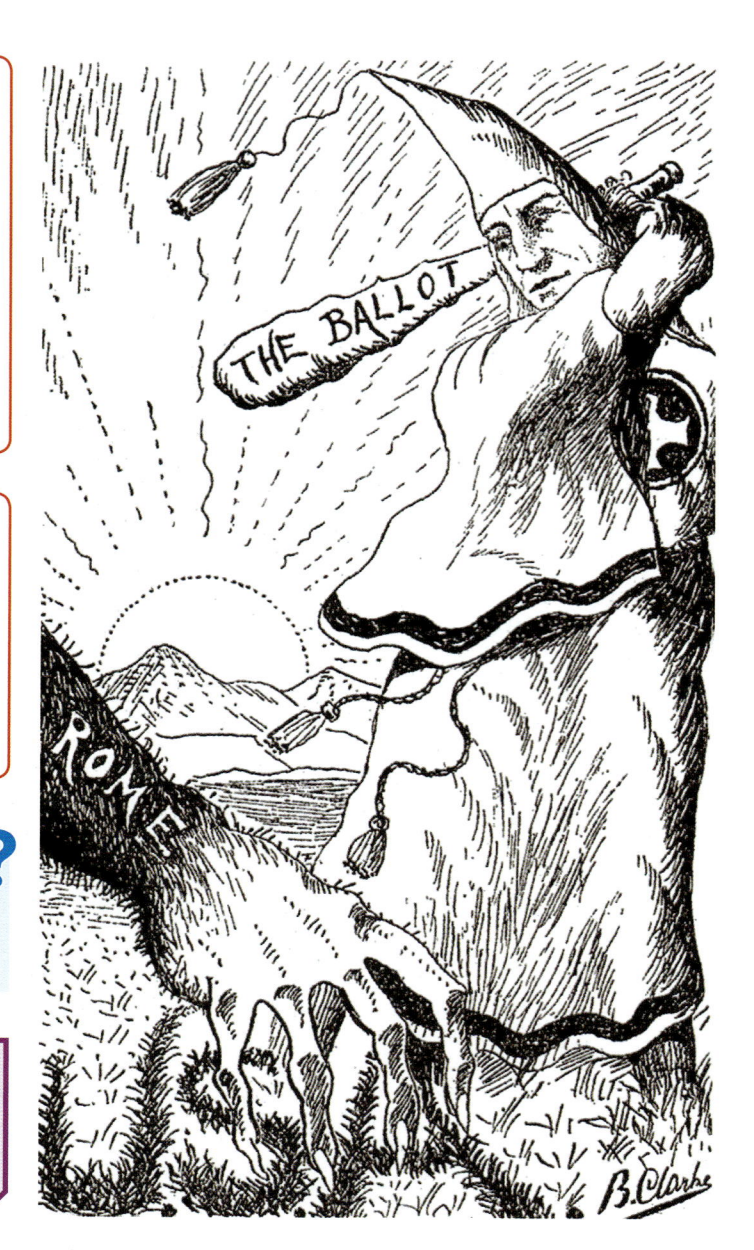

▲ **Source K:** A cartoon published in the *Heroes of the Fiery Cross*, a magazine of the Pillar of Fire Church during the presidential campaign of 1928. The Democrat candidate, Alfred Smith, was Roman Catholic. The Pillar of Fire Church was closely linked to the Ku Klux Klan in the 1920s

Black reaction: Migration

Faced by racism and living in often chronic poverty, thousands of black Americans moved to the cities of the north in the years after 1910, hoping to find a better life. In the years 1916–20, almost 1 million black Americans left the south for jobs in the north. This became known as '**the Great Migration**'.

However, conditions were not much better in the north. Black Americans were given low-paid jobs and were the first to be laid off in bad times. They generally lived in squalid tenement ghettos and faced even more racial intolerance. In New York and Chicago they often lived in poorer housing than whites and yet paid higher rents. They had poorer education and health services than whites.

There was some progress: for example, the Ford Motor Company which was based in the northern industrial cities of Pittsburgh and Detroit employed only 50 black Americans in 1916 but by 1926 it employed 10,000. Nevertheless, the majority of black Americans did not benefit from the economic **boom** of the 1920s.

Northern white Americans frequently objected to the arrival of southern black Americans and feared the competition for jobs and housing. Racial tension grew and in 1919 there were race riots in more than 20 US cities, which resulted in 62 deaths and hundreds of injuries. The worst riots were in Chicago and Washington DC where the army had to be used to restore order. In Chicago, 38 people died, including 15 white and 23 black Americans, and 537 people were injured.

Improvements

However, there were some improvements for black Americans, especially in the northern states.

- In Chicago and New York there was a growing black middle class. In Chicago in 1930 blacks boycotted department stores until they agreed to employ black assistants.
- Jazz brought fame to several black singers and musicians such as Louis Armstrong.
- The black neighbourhood of Harlem in New York became the centre of the Harlem Renaissance for black singers, musicians, artists, writers and poets.
- Black theatre attracted big audiences while black performing artists, including singers, comedians and dancers, were popular in clubs and musical shows.
- Life expectancy for blacks increased from 45 in 1900 to 48 in 1930.

> **Source L:** From an article published in a newspaper for black Americans, 1921
>
> Look around at your cabin, look at the dirt floor and the windows without glass. Then ask your folks already up North about the bathrooms with hot and cold water. What chance has the average black man to get these back home? And if he does get them, how can he be sure that some night some poor white man won't get his gang together and come round and drive him out?

▼ Source M: Urban black population, 1920–30

City	1920	1930	Percentage increase
New York	152,467	327,706	114.9
Chicago	109,458	233,903	113.7
Philadelphia	134,229	219,599	63.6
Detroit	40,838	120,066	194.0
Los Angeles	15,579	38,894	149.7

ACTIVITIES

1. What reasons are given in Source L to explain why many black Americans decided to migrate north?
2. Study Source M. What does it tell you about black American migration in the 1920s?
3. Did life improve for those blacks who did migrate north? Explain your answer.

Practice question

Describe how lives for some black Americans did improve during the 1920s. (For guidance, see page 161.)

Black reaction: the NAACP and the UNIA

Two organisations attempted to draw attention to the unfair treatment of black Americans: the National Association for the Advancement of Colored People (NAACP) and the Universal Negro Improvement Association (UNIA).

National Association for the Advancement of Colored People (NAACP)

William Edward Burghardt, 'W.E.B.', Du Bois set up the **National Association for the Advancement of Colored People (NAACP)** in 1909. He wanted America to accept all people, with equal opportunities for all. By 1919, the NAACP had 90,000 members in 300 branches. The NAACP concentrated on legal methods to fight segregation, using non-violent activities such as marches, demonstrations and petitions. Du Bois campaigned for non-discrimination and the integration of people of all races into a USA that would have equal opportunities for all. Du Bois used the NAACP to challenge white supremacy, especially the segregation laws. He made black Americans much more aware of their civil rights, especially the right to vote. The NAACP also campaigned against the practice of lynching in the south. It investigated and publicised the number of lynchings. Although the NAACP failed to get a law passed banning lynchings, the publicity led to a great reduction in the number being carried out.

W.E.B. DU BOIS (1868–1963)

1868 Born in Massachusetts
1885–88 Educated at Fisk University
1888–92 Attended Harvard University
1892–94 Studied at University of Berlin
1897 Took a professorship in history and economics at Atlanta University
1909 Co-founded the NAACP
1910 Became editor of NAACP's monthly magazine, *The Crisis*
1934 Resigned from the NAACP in a dispute over policy and direction
1944 Returned to the NAACP but dismissed in 1948
1961 Settled in Ghana and joined the American Communist party

▲ Figure 2.2: W.E.B. Du Bois

2 Religion and race

Universal Negro Improvement Association (UNIA)

Marcus Garvey set up the **Universal Negro Improvement Association (UNIA)** in 1914. By 1920 the UNIA had 2,000 members and at its peak, it had about 250,000 members. Marcus Garvey thought that black people should not try to be part of white society. He insisted that they should celebrate their blackness and their African past. The UNIA used more militant tactics than the NAACP. Garvey encouraged black people to set up their own businesses employing only black workers. He encouraged black Americans to return to Africa (his slogan was 'Back to Africa') to 'establish a country and a government on their own'. However, in 1925 Garvey was put in prison for 'postal fraud' and, on his release, he was deported to Jamaica. The UNIA subsequently fell apart. Nevertheless, he passed on the idea taken up by the **Black Power Movement** of the 1960s that 'black is beautiful'.

MARCUS GARVEY (1887–1940)

- **1887** Born in Jamaica
- **1914** Founded the UNIA
- **1916** Moved to Harlem, New York
- **1919** Founded the Black Star Line to provide transportation to Africa, and the Negro Factories Corporation to encourage black economic independence
- **1922** Arrested for fraud, sent to prison and deported to Jamaica
- **1935** Moved to live in London

▲ Figure 2.3: Marcus Garvey in his flamboyant uniform decorated with plumage, brass buttons, braid and sword

ACTIVITIES

1. How did W. E. B. Du Bois and Marcus Garvey differ in their views about how best to help black Americans?
2. Which organisation did more to help improve the lives of black Americans – the NAACP or the UNIA? Give reasons to support your answer.

Practice questions

1. Describe how the NAACP and UNIA attempted to improve the lives of black Americans during the 1920s. *(For guidance, see pages 161.)*
2. Were the Jim Crow laws the worst examples of intolerance in the USA between 1910 and 1929? Use your own knowledge and understanding of the issue to support your answer. *(For guidance, see pages 166–167.)*

3 Crime and corruption

The 1920s was an unsettling decade for the USA and its citizens. It was a time of great prosperity for many and poverty for others. There was racial tension and bigotry which often led to violence. However, the decade is most often remembered for gangsters such as Al Capone and the period of **Prohibition**. Gangsters brought much corruption and violence to the cities of the USA, one of the worst examples being the St Valentine's Day Massacre in Chicago. In some cases whole cities were controlled by them, with police officers, judges and even city mayors under the pay of powerful gangsters. Nor did people see cases of corruption only in the cities; they also saw it in the federal government under the presidency of Warren Harding in the years 1919–23. The feeling grew that morals had deteriorated in the USA and that many people were prepared to break the law. This was clearly demonstrated in the Teapot Dome Scandal of 1922.

Reasons for Prohibition

During the nineteenth century, there had been many groups in the USA who had supported the idea of prohibiting the sale of alcohol. The Women's Christian Temperance Union (1873) and **Anti-Saloon League** (1895) were very powerful organisations and they made the idea of Prohibition one of the top political issues.

Momentum for Prohibition had been building up and this is shown by the fact that, in the years 1906–19, 26 states in the USA passed laws to limit the sale of alcohol. Female reformers had argued for some time that there were clear links between the consumption of alcohol and wife beating and child abuse. Henry Ford and other **industrialists** were concerned that drinking reduced efficiency and output at work. Many religious groups saw alcohol as the root of sin and evil and were keen to support Prohibition. It was felt that Prohibition would support and strengthen the traditional values of the American people, who were God-fearing, hard-working, family-orientated and thrifty. Moreover, it would encourage immigrants to follow these values.

America's participation in the First World War created many problems around the issue of Prohibition. Many brewers were of German origin and when the USA declared war on Germany, the **Temperance Movement** and the Anti-Saloon League saw prohibiting the sale of alcohol as patriotic. Their followers viewed the sale and consumption of alcohol as a betrayal of the USA. As anti-German feeling grew in the USA, beer was given the nickname 'the Kaiser's brew' (the Kaiser was the German emperor).

Source A: Part of a song written in 1903, called 'When the Prohibs Win the Day'

There'll be plenty of food for eating, There'll be plenty of clothes for wear, There'll be gladness in ev'ry meeting, There'll be praise to outmeasure prayer, There'll be toys each day for baby, And then Papa at home will stay, And a heaven on earth will the bright home be, When the Prohibs win the day.

▲ **Source B:** A poster issued by the Anti-Saloon League in 1917 to highlight the evils of alcohol

3 Crime and corruption

In September 1918, President Woodrow Wilson banned beer production until the war ended. There was little opposition to this move – there were not even any organised bodies to counter the arguments of the Prohibition lobby. The Prohibition Amendment, which stopped the 'manufacture, sale or transportation of intoxicating liquors' was ratified in Congress in January 1919 and was scheduled to come into effect one year later. The amendment did not outlaw buying or drinking alcohol, nor did it define the term 'intoxicating liquors'. In 1920, Congress passed the Volstead Act which defined 'intoxicating liquors' as anything containing more than 0.5 per cent alcohol. The Internal Revenue Service (IRS) became responsible for enforcing Prohibition.

Source E: From an Anti-Saloon League pamphlet, 1918
The American's patriotic duty is to abolish the un-American, pro-German, crime-producing, food-wasting, youth-corrupting, home-wrecking, treasonable liquor traffic.

ACTIVITIES

1 What do Sources B and E suggest about American attitudes to alcohol?
2 Use Source A and your own knowledge to explain why there was support for Prohibition.
3 Copy and complete the mind map to show why Prohibition was introduced.

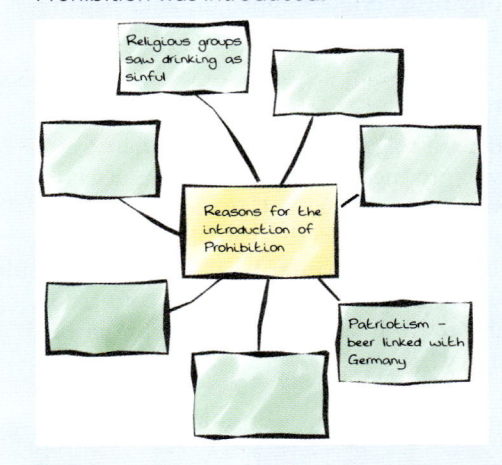

▲ **Source C:** A cartoon published in a US newspaper during the First World War

Practice questions

1 What was the purpose of Source C? *(For guidance, see pages 162–163.)*
2 Describe how the different groups within American society campaigned for the introduction of Prohibition. *(For guidance, see page 161.)*

▼ **Source D:** Women demonstrating in favour of Prohibition in Madison, Minnesota, 1917

Life under Prohibition

Prohibition drove drinkers and drinking underground. It became impossible to prevent people from drinking alcohol – and crucially from drinking beverages with an alcoholic content of greater than 0.5 per cent. Huge numbers of people were prepared to break the law not only to produce alcohol but to go to private bars to consume it. For many ordinary people, consuming alcohol or visiting a 'speakeasy' did not feel like breaking the law. Prohibition created a situation where consumers wanted a product which could not be provided by legitimate means. To satisfy this demand, organised crime stepped in. Thus began the age of the gangster.

Smuggling

It was never difficult to get hold of alcohol. There were many people who produced it illegally and many who smuggled it from Europe, Mexico, Canada and the Caribbean. The USA had more than 30,000 kilometres of coastline and land borders to guard, and so it was difficult to prevent the smuggling of alcohol into the country. It was even possible to find doctors who would prescribe 'medicinal whiskey'.

PROHIBITION TERMS

Speakeasy	illegal drinking saloon
Bootlegger	one who produced or sold alcohol illegally
Bathtub gin	home-brewed gin
Still	a device for distilling alcohol
Moonshine	illegally distilled or smuggled alcohol
Rum runner	someone who illegally transports liquor across a border

ACTIVITIES

1. Study Source F. What does it tell you about Prohibition?
2. How successful was the US government in preventing the smuggling of alcohol into the country?

◀ **Source F:** This 1920s' cartoon shows Uncle Sam and a man labelled 'State' arguing, each demanding of the other, 'You do it!' In the background a smiling 'bootlegger' stands next to boxes labelled 'Gin', 'Beer', 'Choice Liquor' and 'Handmade Liquor'

Speakeasies

Within a short time after the introduction of Prohibition, there were more speakeasies than there had been legal saloons in the old days. In New York alone there were more than 30,000 speakeasies by 1930. An owner of a speakeasy had many overheads. As well as purchasing the illegal alcohol, they would have to pay off the federal agents, senior police officers, city officials (and also the police on the beat when deliveries were made). This situation was replicated across the USA.

Health

Prohibition had mixed consequences for the health of Americans. Deaths from alcoholism had fallen by 80 per cent by 1921, but by 1926 about 50,000 people had died from poisoned alcohol. Male deaths from cirrhosis of the liver fell from 29.5 per 100,000 in 1911 to 10.7 per 100,000 in 1929, yet doctors reported an increase in cases of blindness and paralysis – again as a result of drinking poisoned alcohol. Many pointed out that Prohibition reduced the number of people killed on the roads and the incidence of drink-related accidents at work did diminish. Moreover, per capita consumption of alcohol fell during Prohibition.

ACTIVITY

Use Source G and your own knowledge to explain why some Americans wanted to end Prohibition.

Source G: A speech given by Pauline Sabin in 1929 in which she calls for the repeal of Prohibition. Sabin founded the Women's Organisation for National Prohibition Reform in Chicago in 1929

In pre-Prohibition days, mothers had little fear in regard to the saloon as far as their children were concerned. A saloon-keeper's license was revoked if he was caught selling liquor to minors. Today in any speakeasy in the United States you can find boys and girls in their teens drinking liquor and this situation has become so acute that the mothers of the country feel something must be done to protect their children.

The brewing industry

Prohibition had a lasting effect on the nation's brewing industry. St Louis had 22 breweries before Prohibition. Only nine re-opened after Prohibition ended in 1933. The Anheuser-Busch company survived only because it diversified into soft drinks, developed a bottling industry and even manufactured car and lorry parts. In 1915, there were 1,345 breweries in the USA. In 1934, there were only 756.

Practice questions

1. Describe how Prohibition was openly ignored across many parts of America. *(For guidance, see page 161.)*
2. Use Source H and your own knowledge to describe the role of the speakeasy in the 1920s. *(For guidance, see pages 159–160.)*

▲ **Source H:** A speakeasy in the mid-1920s showing a flapper smuggling the illegal alcohol

The enforcement of Prohibition

ACTIVITIES

1. Explain why it was difficult to enforce Prohibition.
2. Study Source J. What does it show you about the ending of Prohibition?

Enforcing Prohibition proved impossible. The Internal Revenue Service (IRS) never had more than 2,500 agents and some of them became paid hands of the gang leaders. The most famous of the IRS agents was Eliot Ness, the man who eventually arrested Al Capone (see page 123). Most Americans were prepared to break the Prohibition law, and so a new criminal age began. Making and selling alcohol brought profits. Police and city officials were aware of the spread of speakeasies and bootleggers, but the lawbreakers realised that bribery would buy silence. One New York politician said it would take 250,000 federal agents to enforce Prohibition and that hundreds more would be needed to check the police. What followed in the 1920s was a growth of public corruption on a scale never before seen in the USA.

The end of Prohibition

By the late 1920s there was growing opposition to Prohibition. Many anti-Prohibition groups had been formed to highlight the alcohol-related problems caused by the trade in illegal alcohol. As a result of such campaigning the Prohibition law was abolished in December 1933. It marked the end of the age of the bootlegger.

Practice question

What was the purpose of Source I? *(For guidance, see pages 162–163.)*

Source I: A cartoon, published in the late 1920s, showing Uncle Sam exhausted by the devil's flow of bootleg liquor

Source J: People in New York celebrating the end of Prohibition, December 1933

3 Crime and corruption

Organised crime

There were criminal gangs in the USA before Prohibition, but the 1920s saw a rapid growth in their power. Prohibition gave criminals the opportunities to broaden their involvement in such activities as bootlegging. The gangs bought out hundreds of breweries and transported illegal beer in armoured lorries. Gang leaders saw themselves as businessmen and when faced with competition they took over their rivals. However, the takeovers were often carried out violently and usually ended with the murder of the opposition. Gangs frequently used the Thompson sub-machine gun, which was nicknamed the 'Chicago Piano' and the 'Chicago Typewriter'.

Gangs were involved in what were known as **rackets**, for example, protection, prostitution, 'numbers' (illegal lottery).

AL CAPONE 1899–1947

1899	Born in New York
1917	Joins the Five Points Gang led by Johnny Torrio
1921	Moves to Chicago to work with Torrio
1922	Partner in Torrio's saloons, gambling houses and brothels
1925	Takes over operations when Torrio leaves Chicago
1929	Is responsible for the St Valentine's Day Massacre
1931	Is indicted for **income tax** evasion and found guilty as charged
1939	Wins release from prison
1947	Dies in Palm Island, Florida

Al Capone

Al Capone epitomises the gangster of the Prohibition era. The son of Italian immigrants, he left school at an early age and became involved in small-time criminal activities. Capone was given the nickname 'Scarface' following a fight when he was a bouncer at a New York club. His links to the crook Johnny Torrio led him to Chicago where he eventually rose through the ranks to take over Torrio's operations. Capone cemented his position as one of the leading gangsters in Chicago by bribing local officials. Before long, he had half of the city's employees on his payroll.

Capone controlled the mayor 'Big Bill' Thompson and senior police officers, and fixed local elections. In Chicago, he controlled speakeasies, bookmakers' joints, gambling houses, brothels, horse and race tracks, nightclubs, distilleries and breweries. He drove around in a bullet-proof Cadillac, which always contained his bodyguards who were armed with machine guns. In order to ensure that he controlled Chicago, Capone had more than 200 of his rivals killed in the years 1925–29. There were no convictions for any of these murders.

Despite his criminal activities, Capone was seen by many Americans as a glamorous person. He moved in the highest social circles and 'put Chicago on the map'. He was the first to open soup kitchens after the 1929 **Wall Street Crash** (see Source L) and he ordered stores to give clothes and food to the needy at his own expense.

Source K: A description of an election in Cicero, a suburb of Chicago, from a local newspaper, 1924

Cars filled with gunmen paraded the streets slugging and kidnapping election workers. Polling places were raided by armed thugs and ballots taken at the point of a gun from the hands of voters waiting to drop them in the box. Voters and workers were kidnapped, taken to Chicago and held prisoners until the polls closed.

ACTIVITIES

1. What does Source K suggest about the power exercised by some gangsters?
2. a) Study Source L. Write a newspaper headline for the source.
   b) Suggest reasons why Capone opened soup kitchens for the unemployed.

◀ **Source L:** Big Al's soup kitchen, Chicago 1930. The soup kitchen was set up for unemployed workers by Al Capone

123

The St Valentine's Day Massacre

In his quest for the control of all gangs, Capone was involved in the infamous St Valentine's Day Massacre. On 14 February 1929, Bugs Moran, the leader of a rival Chicago gang, narrowly escaped death but seven of his men were machine-gunned in a garage by Capone's men who entered the building dressed as police officers. Capone himself was in Florida with the perfect alibi. It was this incident which made many Americans realise that the gangsters, and Capone in particular, were not the glamorous characters they had imagined.

Arrest

In 1931, Capone was prosecuted for income tax evasion for the years 1925–29. It was claimed that he owed more than $200,000 in taxes from gambling profits. He was subsequently found guilty and his role as gang leader was over. The demise of Capone seemed to herald the end of the age of the gangster. With the Depression setting in, the American people had plenty of other issues to contend with.

ACTIVITIES

1. Explain why gangsters were responsible for an increase in violent crime during the 1920s.
2. Working in pairs, design your own poster for a film glamorising the gangster age.

Practice questions

1. Use Source M and your own knowledge to describe the St Valentine's Day Massacre. *(For guidance, see pages 159–160.)*
2. Describe how Al Capone became Chicago's chief gangster. *(For guidance, see page 161.)*
3. Describe the events which led to the arrest and prosecution of Al Capone. *(For guidance, see page 161.)*

Source M: The front page of *The Chicago Daily News* newspaper carrying the news of the St Valentine's Day Massacre

Corruption

President Harding and the 'Ohio Gang'

Just as there was corruption in towns and cities in the USA during Prohibition, there were examples of corruption in the government in Washington DC.

In 1919 the new president, Warren Harding, promised the USA that there would be a return to 'normalcy' after the distress caused by the First World War. Harding surrounded himself in his cabinet with friends and colleagues, many of whom were from Ohio and who were collectively given the nickname the 'Ohio Gang'. However, some of Harding's friends used their position to line their pockets with money. The Head of the Veterans' Bureau was fined and sent to jail for selling off veterans' hospital supplies for personal profit. Another colleague resigned in disgrace and two more committed suicide rather than face a public disgrace over the scandal.

Harry Daugherty 1860–1941
- 1881 Qualified as lawyer
- 1890–94 Republican member of Ohio legislature
- 1920 Leader of Republican Party in Ohio
- 1921–24 Attorney-General
- 1924 Resigned as Attorney-General

President Warren Harding 1865–1923
- 1900–04 Republican member of Ohio legislature
- 1904–06 Lieutenant-Governor of Ohio
- 1915–21 Senator for Ohio
- 1921–23 President

Albert Fall 1861–1944
- 1891 Qualified as a lawyer
- 1893 Appointed judge in New Mexico
- 1912 Republican Senator for New Mexico
- 1921 Appointed Secretary of the Interior by Harding
- 1923 Resigned
- 1929 Imprisoned for one year over the Teapot Dome Scandal

Figure 3.1: Members of President Warren Harding's cabinet, 1921

Edwin Denby (1870–1929)
- 1896 Graduated in law from Michigan University and began work as a lawyer
- 1905–11 Republican delegate for Michigan in US House of Representatives
- 1917–20 Served in US Marine Corps, rising to rank of major
- 1921–24 Secretary of the Navy under Harding and Coolidge
- 1924 Resigned from office over the Teapot Dome Scandal
- 1924 Went back to practising law

Charles Forbes (1878–1952)
- 1916 Harding met Forbes in Hawaii where Forbes was in charge of building a naval base at Pearl Habor
- 1921–23 Appointed by Harding as the first Director of the Veteran's Bureau where he embezzled government funds
- 1923 Following accusations of corruption he resigned from office and fled to Europe
- 1925 Put on trial, accused of taking $200 million from government funds
- 1926 Found guilty and given a two-year prison sentence; he was released after one year

Thomas Miller (1886–1973)
- 1908 Graduated in law from Yale University
- 1913–15 Served as Secretary of State for Delaware
- 1915–17 Republican delegate for Delaware in US House of Representatives
- 1921 Appointed by Harding as Alien Property Custodian, a post he held until 1925
- 1927 Convicted of defrauding the US government and served 18 months in prison
- 1933 Pardoned by President Hoover

The Teapot Dome Scandal

Harding and his government were disgraced even more with the so-called Teapot Dome Scandal. Albert Fall, Harding's Secretary of the Interior, leased government oil fields to wealthy friends in exchange for hundreds of thousands of dollars in bribes. The oil fields were to be specifically used for the US navy following a decision in Congress in 1920 to ensure that there would always be sufficient reserves in times of a national emergency. Harry Sinclair (Head of Mammoth Oil Company) obtained leases to drill for oil at Teapot Dome, Wyoming, and Edward Doheny (owner of the Pan-American Petroleum and Transport Company) acquired leases for reserves at Elk Hills, California. Fall received about $400,000 in cash and gifts from Doheny and Sinclair. The deals were secret but when Fall began spending large amounts of money, suspicions grew about how he had come by it. By the time he had finished leasing the navy's reserves, Fall had given Sinclair and Doheny oil reserves which were estimated to be worth $100 million. He himself had collected from them $409,000 in cash and bonds.

Some details of the deals were published in newspapers in April 1922 and President Harding defended the actions of Fall saying that he had, in fact, approved them. At first, Fall's leasing of the oil deposits seemed unimportant. When asked about the secrecy of the arrangements, Fall replied that national security required it. Doheny similarly claimed patriotism and security to justify his actions. However, there was an outcry from many leading US oil companies because they had not been able to bid openly for the leases. The Senate began to demand an investigation and Harding became so distressed by the events that he fell ill and contracted pneumonia. At the height of the crisis, President Harding said: 'I have no trouble with my enemies. I can take care of them. It is my friends that are giving me trouble.' Harding died in August 1923 and was succeeded by Calvin Coolidge, who was gradually able to restore faith in the government.

Senator Thomas Walsh, a Democrat from Montana, led the Senate's investigation. He was criticised by many newspapers and Republicans for his sensationalism during the investigation. He was also harassed by the FBI who tapped his phones, opened his mail and made anonymous threats to his life. The Senate inquiry dragged on for several years and finally, in 1927, the **Supreme Court** ruled that the oil leases had been corruptly obtained and invalidated the leases. The navy regained control of the Teapot Dome and Elk Hills reserves. Albert Fall was found guilty of bribery in 1929, fined $100,000 and sentenced to one year in prison. He became the first ever US government official to be imprisoned. Harry Sinclair, who refused to co-operate with the government investigators, was charged with contempt and received a short sentence for tampering with the jury. Edward Doheny was acquitted in 1930 of the attempt to bribe Fall.

During the inquiry Harry Daugherty, the Attorney-General, was himself accused of obstructing investigations and was forced to resign in 1924.

ACTIVITIES

1. How corrupt was government under President Harding?
2. Explain why there was a scandal over events at Teapot Dome.
3. Can you suggest reasons why Senator Walsh was harassed during the Teapot Dome investigation?

Practice questions

1. What was the purpose of Source N? *(For guidance, see pages 162–163.)*
2. Was organised crime the biggest problem facing American society during the 1920s? Use your own knowledge and understanding of the issue to support your answer. *(For guidance, see pages 166–167.)*

◀ **Source N:** A cartoon that appeared in an American newspaper in 1922 showing the Teapot Dome Scandal. One of the figures running away is Albert Fall

4 Economic boom

The USA greatly benefited economically from the First World War and, in the 1920s, experienced an economic boom. The boom was due to the availability of natural resources and a cheap labour force as well as advanced techniques of mass-production used by the car industry, which were then copied in other industries. There was a rapid growth in newer industries fuelled by electrification and by the availability of easy **credit** through **hire purchase**. These factors caused a growth in demand which in turn resulted in a dramatic rise in the values of **stocks and shares** on the US **stock market**, helping to enable the country to experience an economic boom. This was encouraged by the policies of successive Republican presidents who placed an emphasis on their beliefs in laissez-faire, individualism and protectionism.

America's economic position in 1910

The US economic boom was in part the result of America's natural resources and assets, notably its cheap labour supply. A boom occurs when the economy of a country is rapidly developing. Factories make and sell a lot of goods which, in turn, make money that is put back into factories, to make and sell goods and make even more money. In other words, an economy experiences the multiplier effect, whereby the growth of one industry benefits and stimulates the growth of another. For example, in the USA in this period:

- The growth of the car industry benefited the rubber and glass industries.
- The development of electricity stimulated the growth of new industries which made electrical products such as vacuum cleaners and fridges.

Natural resources

The USA had a plentiful supply of raw materials which included oil, coal, wood and iron. These resources had provided the foundation for US economic growth in the years before the First World War and stimulated further growth in the 1920s.

Cheap labour force

There was continuous immigration from Europe to the USA in the years before the First World War (see Source A). This provided a plentiful supply of cheap, unskilled labour from Germany, Scandinavia, Italy, Poland, Russia, Ireland, China and Japan.

▶ **Source A:** This cartoon from 1880 shows a figure representing the USA and immigrants arriving in the USA

127

The economic impact of the First World War

The USA did not enter the First World War until April 1917. Its economy benefited greatly from the war. Indeed, by 1918 the USA was the world's leading economy.

- The war was fought in Europe and badly affected the economies of leading countries such as Britain, France and Germany, who had to divert their resources to the war effort.
- These countries bought much-needed supplies from the USA. Money poured into the USA for food, raw materials and **munitions**. This led to the growth of US industry and agriculture.
- Many countries ended up borrowing huge sums of money from the USA. American bankers and businessmen increasingly invested in Europe and made money once the economies of these countries recovered in the 1920s.
- In addition, during the war, European countries were unable to maintain their pre-war export levels. USA manufacturers and farmers took over European overseas markets and further expanded (see Figure 4.1). For example, the USA took over from Germany as the leading producer in the world for fertilisers and chemicals.
- The war stimulated technological advances, especially **mechanisation**, as well as the development of new raw materials such as plastics. As a result, the USA led the world in new technology.

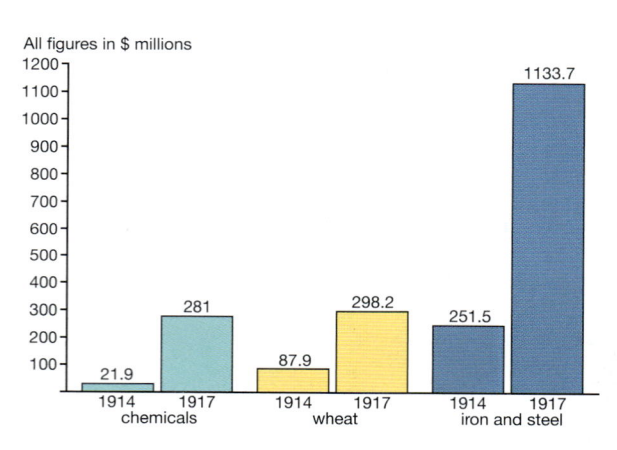

▲ Figure 4.1: American exports, 1914–17

▲ **Source B:** An American factory making shells and munitions during the First World War

ACTIVITIES

1. Explain why the American economy was able to grow during the period 1910–19.
2. What information does Figure 4.1 provide about American exports during period of the First World War?
3. Study Source A. How did the arrival of so many immigrants help the American economy during this period?

Practice question

Use Source B and your own knowledge to describe the impact of the First World War on the American economy. *(For guidance, see pages 159–160.)*

4 Economic boom

Electrification

At the start of the 1920s, the USA experienced another industrial revolution. One reason for this was widespread use of electrical power. Electricity had developed slowly before the war but the amount of electricity consumed more than doubled during the 1920s. In 1912, only 16 per cent of the American people lived in electrically lit homes. By 1927, the number had risen to 63 per cent. Most homes in the cities had electricity by the end of the decade.

The development of electricity was fundamental to industrial growth. It provided a cheaper, more reliable, efficient and flexible form of power for factories, workshops and other industries. More and more factories were run by electricity and the growth of electric power encouraged a much more widespread use of electrical goods. The electrification of the USA brought about the development of a whole range of domestic goods including radios, gramophones, telephones, washing machines, vacuum cleaners, cookers and refrigerators. For example:

- In 1926, Hoover introduced the famous 'beats-as-it-sweeps-as-it-cleans' vacuum cleaner, which cleverly incorporated the three established methods of cleaning carpets: beating, sweeping and suction cleaning. This innovation set the standard for the rest of the market to follow.
- By 1900, half of American houses were using an icebox to keep food cold. The ice used for storage was expensive so the remaining households had very little in the way of cooled storage. That all changed when General Electric developed the first Monitor-Top unit in 1927. This was the first refrigerator to be used over a large area.

Nevertheless, it is also important to recognise that consumption of other energy sources also grew during this period; for example, the amount of oil used doubled, and usage of gas quadrupled.

ACTIVITY QUESTION

How important was the increase in electrical power to the growth of the US economy in the 1920s?

Practice question

Use Source C and your own knowledge to describe the growth of American industry during the 1920s. *(For guidance, see pages 159–160.)*

▲ **Source C:** Cartoon showing a tiny Uncle Sam admiring his industrial might

Mass production

Much of industry was becoming modernised in the USA in the period 1910–29. More industries employed modern manufacturing techniques such as **mass production**. During the 1920s mass production techniques were used in many industries, such as household goods and textiles. For example, the introduction of standard clothing sizes across the whole of the USA during the First World War made it possible to mass produce clothing. Mass production was also established in the manufacture of firearms, sewing machines and railway engines. They were later extended to the production of clocks, typewriters and bicycles.

The car industry played a very important role in the boom of the 1920s, often leading the way in technological change as well as stimulating the growth of other industries. Mass production techniques adopted by the car industry sped up industrial production, improved productivity and led to greater profits.

The assembly line

Mass production was based on moving assembly lines. This process was most famously developed by motor vehicle manufacturer Henry Ford. In 1913, the motor company Ford introduced the much more efficient method of producing the cars, the assembly line or 'magic belt'. Henry Ford had seen how efficiently this was used in meat-packing factories and slaughterhouses. An electric conveyor belt carried the partly assembled car at the same speed past workers who stood at the same spot and did one job, such as fitting on the wheels or doors. This saved time as the tools and equipment were brought to the worker rather than him having to waste time walking about for them. In 1913, the Ford factory in Detroit was producing one car every three minutes. By 1920, the same factory was producing the same car every ten seconds.

> **Source D:** Henry Ford describes an assembly line in the mid-1920s
>
> In the chassis assembly line there are 45 separate operations. Some men do only two small operations, others do more. The man who places the part does not fasten it. The man who puts the bolt in does not put the nut on and the man who puts the nut on does not tighten it. On operation 34 the motor gets its petrol. On operation 44 the radiator is filled with water and on operation 45 the car drives onto the road.

HENRY FORD (1863–1947)

Henry Ford was an electrical engineer who built his first car in a rented brick shed. In 1903 he founded the Ford Motor Company in Detroit. In 1908 he introduced his Ford Model T, which was nicknamed the 'Tin Lizzie'. Existing car manufacturers built several different models in a range of colours. Ford showed the benefits (and reduced costs) of manufacturing one standard model which was 'any colour as long as it was black'.

Ford believed in hard work and would walk round his factory each day encouraging his workers to do their job properly. However, he had quite a turnover of workers who found the assembly line boring and monotonous. Therefore, in 1914, Ford announced that he would double the wages to $5 a day, which was far more than anyone else paid for the equivalent job. Workers rushed to Detroit to work for him. He also reduced the length of the working day to eight hours and introduced a third shift, so the factory was operating a three-shift system and working 24 hours each day.

Ford was also prepared to use modern advertising techniques to sell his cars. For example, he realised the value of using attractive women in adverts, not only because it would encourage men to buy his cars, but also to promote the idea of female drivers.

The effect of mass production on the car industry

Mass production allowed Ford to bring down the price of cars and so make them affordable for many more Americans. In 1914 a Model T cost $850. By 1926, the price had dropped to $295. Owning a car was no longer just a rich person's privilege, as it was in Europe in the mid-1920s.

Mass production therefore made the automobile far more accessible: between 1920 and 1929 the numbers of cars rose from 7.5 million to 27 million. Cars prompted Americans to see more of their homeland and as a result, greater tourism and hotels developed. Mass production of cars also stimulated road building at the rate of 10,000 miles per year by 1929.

ACTIVITIES

1. Explain how the introduction of the assembly line helped to increase the production of cars in Henry Ford's factories.
2. How important was the car industry to the development of the American economy during the 1920s?

Practice question

Use Source E and your own knowledge to describe the impact of mass production on life in America. *(For guidance, see pages 159–160.)*

▲ **Source E:** Ford Model Ts on a high street in the USA in the mid-1920s

How did developments in the new consumer society contribute to the economic boom?

Consumerism

As profits increased, so did wages (though by nothing like so much). Between 1923 and 1929, the average wage rose by eight per cent. Though this was not spectacular, it was enough to enable some workers to buy – often on credit (also called hire purchase) – new consumer luxuries (see Figure 4.2). The development of advertising and radio commercials in the 1920s, such as the advert in Source G, encouraged people to buy these new goods.

Advertising

The advertising industry also grew rapidly as more and more firms realised the potential of the advert for increasing sales and profits. The industry used quite sophisticated techniques with more colourful adverts and the use of catchphrases. Although magazines and newspapers remained the most important method, the radio and cinema provided a whole range of new opportunities.

The people who designed the advertisements studied the psychology of the consumer and devised methods that they believed would encourage people to buy their products. Women were not only used to advertise many goods, they were also targets for the advertisers (see Source F).

> **Source F:** The manager of an advertising firm explained how to appeal to women. He made these comments in 1926
>
> Nine-tenths of the goods bought annually are bought by women. Woman is a creature of the imagination. We pay her a compliment when we say this, for imagination comes from the feelings and feelings come from the heart. And so the advertising appeal, to reach women, must not ignore the first great quality of the heart, which is love. Most advertisers do not ignore the quality of love. There, in almost every advertisement, is a reference, in word or picture, to mother love, to the home, to children, to sentiment.

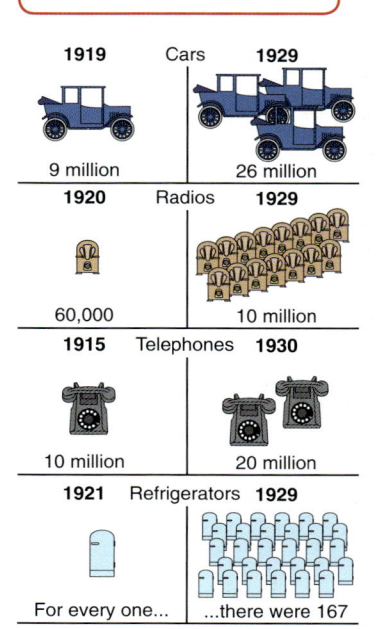

Cars
- 1919: 9 million
- 1929: 26 million

Radios
- 1920: 60,000
- 1929: 10 million

Telephones
- 1915: 10 million
- 1930: 20 million

Refrigerators
- 1921: For every one...
- 1929: ...there were 167

▲ Figure 4.2: Growth in sales of consumer goods

▲ Source G: Advert for a vacuum cleaner in the 1920s

Department stores

The 1920s also saw the growth of department stores as more and more people bought **consumer goods**, especially electrical appliances. In the cities, chain stores stocked the new range of goods now available. In addition, the USA was the first country to have a supermarket. JC Penney opened a chain of supermarkets known as Piggly Wiggly. The first was opened in Memphis, Tennessee, in 1916. Customers helped themselves to the goods, which were individually priced, and paid for them at the checkout as opposed to waiting to be served at the shop counter.

Credit – hire purchase

The growth of credit made it much easier for people to buy goods even when they did not have enough cash to pay for them immediately. Under this system of hire purchase, goods were paid for in instalments. About half the goods sold in the 1920s were paid for by hire purchase.

ACTIVITIES

1. Explain why there was a growth in consumerism in the USA in the 1920s.
2. What does Source F suggest about the methods used by advertisers in the 1920s?
3. Devise a suitable caption that could have been used with Source H to advertise the Piggly Wiggly store.

Practice questions

1. What was the purpose of Source G? *(For guidance, see pages 162–163.)*
2. Describe the growth in ownership of electrical goods during the 1920s. *(For guidance, see page 161.)*

▼ **Source H:** The inside of the first Piggly Wiggly store

Laissez-faire, individualism and protectionism

In the 1920s, all the presidents of the USA were Republicans, which meant that they held similar political and economic views. They were:

- Warren Harding, 1921–23
- Calvin Coolidge, 1923–29
- Herbert Hoover, 1929–33

The attitudes and policies of the Republican presidents contributed to the economic boom. When Harding was elected as president, he promised that he would return the USA '**back to normalcy**'. However, he was president for only two years, dying suddenly in 1923. Directly after his death, it was revealed that he had been involved in financial scandals. Coolidge, who succeeded Harding, carried on the policy of limiting the role of government in the economy and reducing the tax burden on the rich. During Coolidge's time as president, the US economy went through a period of unparalleled growth. Hoover, the president who succeeded Coolidge, was a self-made millionaire and he was the Republicans' best example of what could be achieved in the USA by hard work and little government interference.

Laissez-faire

In 1924, President Coolidge made the comment that 'The business of America is business.' He believed, and it was a view held by many Americans, that governments should be involved as little as possible in the day-to-day running of the economy. If businessmen were left alone to make their own decisions, he thought that high profits, more jobs and good wages would be the result. This was the policy of **laissez-faire** – the only role for the government was to help business when it was asked to.

Under Harding and Coolidge laissez-faire contributed to the prosperity of the USA. Low taxes and few regulations meant that businessmen were able to chase profits without fear of interference.

Individualism

Successive Republican presidents also believed in '**rugged individualism**'. This term was used by Republican presidents such as Hoover who believed that people achieved success by their own hard work. It originates with the early Americans who moved to the West and made a new life for themselves through their own efforts.

Protectionism

In the years after 1919 the USA returned to a policy of **isolationism** and refused to become involved in events abroad, particularly in Europe. Linked with this, the Republican governments put **tariffs** on imported goods in order to limit the competition from foreign imports. Imports became more expensive compared to American-made goods. This, in turn, encouraged the purchase of American goods and helped US-based producers.

However, the government of this period did act twice to intervene in the economy:

- The Fordney–McCumber Tariff (1922) raised **import duties** on goods coming into the USA to the highest level ever, thus protecting American industry and encouraging Americans to buy home-produced goods.
- A reduction of income tax rates left some people with more cash to spend on consumer goods. This, in turn, provided the cash to buy the home-produced goods.

> **ACTIVITY**
>
> How did the economic policies of the Republican governments of the 1920s contribute to the economic boom?

> **Practice question**
>
> Were the policies of the Republican governments of the 1920s the most important reason for the economic boom in the USA? Use your own knowledge and understanding of the issue to support your answer. *(For guidance, see pages 166–167.)*

5 The end of prosperity

In October 1929, the American stock market on **Wall Street** crashed. This was due to long-term problems with the US economy, especially over-production and a fall in consumer demand, together with over-speculation on the stock market which eventually led to the panic selling of shares, the collapse in share prices and the crash of the stock market. The immediate effects of the Wall Street Crash were disastrous for the USA and many countries in Europe, especially Britain and Germany. In America, banks literally went bankrupt, leading to a depression and very high unemployment. The Roaring Twenties had come to an abrupt and, in many cases, unfortunate end.

Long-term reasons for the end of prosperity

In the autumn of 1929, the prices of shares on the US stock market crashed, wiping out the fortunes of many Americans. The Crash ushered in **the Great Depression** of the 1930s – the worst economic decline in the history of the USA. It was a time when millions of Americans could not find work, thousands were turned out of their homes, and many roamed the land in railway wagons. Banks failed and people lost their life's savings.

There were several long-term reasons why the Crash happened in 1929, including:

- over-production
- falling demand for consumer goods
- the boom in land and property values.

Over-production

The problems created by over-production are shown in the diagram to the right.

Over-production

1. Fewer products such as cars being sold.

2. This was partly caused by over-production. Factories had produced more goods than Americans could afford to buy.

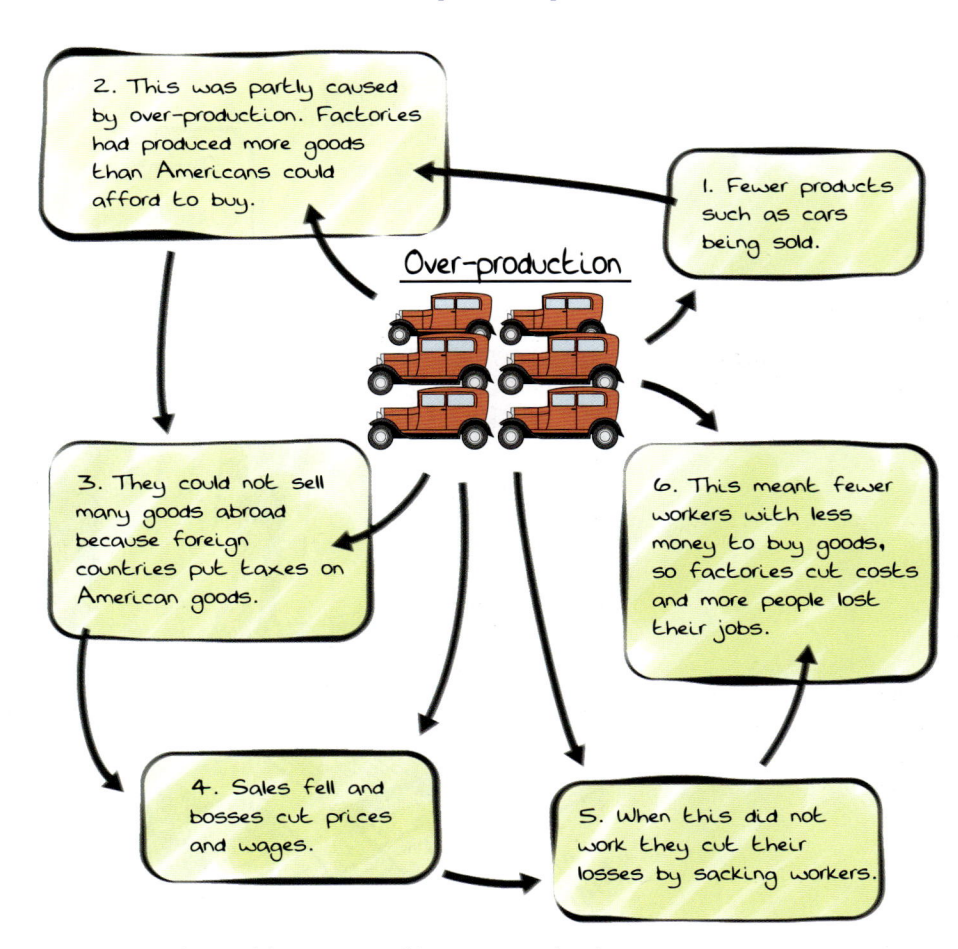

3. They could not sell many goods abroad because foreign countries put taxes on American goods.

4. Sales fell and bosses cut prices and wages.

5. When this did not work they cut their losses by sacking workers.

6. This meant fewer workers with less money to buy goods, so factories cut costs and more people lost their jobs.

▲ Figure 5.1: The problems created by over-production

Falling consumer demand

Several reasons are attributed to the fall in demand for consumer goods.

- The unequal distribution of wealth. The new-found wealth of the 1920s was not shared by everyone. Almost 50 per cent of American families had an income of less than $2,000 a year, the minimum needed to survive. They could not afford to buy the new consumer goods. Some manufacturers did not see that there was a limit to what could be bought, and so they continued to produce goods. The result was over-production.
- The USA could not sell its surplus products to other countries, especially those in Europe. Some European countries owed the USA huge amounts of money and were struggling with repayments. The US government had put high tariffs on foreign goods in the 1920s (see page 134). Many foreign governments responded by doing the same to American goods and consequently US businessmen found it very difficult to sell their goods abroad. Therefore, an ideal outlet for their over-production was blocked.
- During the First World War US banks had lent money to several European countries. These countries found it hard to repay these loans in the 1920s.

The boom in land and property values

One consequence of the increased wealth of the 1920s was a dramatic rise in the value of land and property. The state of Florida witnessed a sharp rise in land values with many speculators attempting to jump on the band wagon and buy property or land. Some people borrowed heavily to do so, believing that they could keep the property for a short time and then sell when it had risen in value. In 1926, however, property prices began to fall sharply in Florida and this left many homeowners in negative equity. This meant that the land or property they owned was worth substantially less than what they had originally paid for it. This was a warning that the US economy was in the process of readjustment, but it was a warning ignored by many investors.

ACTIVITIES

1. What does Sources A suggest about the problems facing the US economy by the late 1920s?
2. How important was over-production in causing an end to the economic boom of the 1920s?

Practice question

Describe the long-term causes of the Wall Street Crash.
(For guidance, see page 161.)

Source A: A cartoon of 1927 showing the problems of mass production

What were the short-term reasons for the end of prosperity?

Short-term reasons for why prosperity came to a sudden end included:

- over-speculation on the stock market
- the availability of easy credit.

Over-speculation

During the 1920s, more and more Americans bought shares on the stock exchange and prices kept rising. In 1928, however, shares did not rise as much as in previous years. This was because many companies were not selling as many goods, so their profits fell. Fewer people were willing to buy their shares and there was a drop in confidence in the market. This was a warning, but when share prices began rising again, greed took over and speculation recurred.

The complete lack of stock market regulation by the government or any other agency encouraged more and more speculation. Successive Republican presidents stuck to their beliefs in laissez-faire. In 1925, the stock market value of stocks stood at $27 billion but by October 1929, it had reached $87 billion. By the summer of 1929 there were 20 million shareholders in the USA and prices continued to rise.

The availability of easy credit

The growth of credit made it much easier for people to buy goods even though they did not have enough cash to pay for them on the spot. Firms arranged for customers to pay in instalments on hire purchase. This included the practice of buying shares on credit, 'on the margin'. This practice was further encouraged by the easy credit policies on the part of the **Federal Reserve Board**.

This worked well as long as prices were rising. However, when the price rise started to slow down or prices fell, problems set in. Seventy-five per cent of the purchase price of shares was borrowed. This, in turn, created artificially high prices.

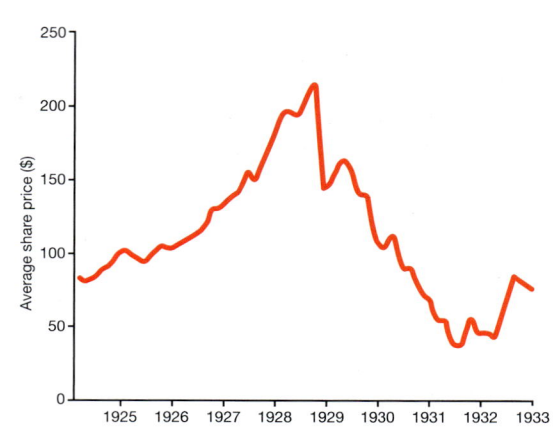

▲ Figure 5.2: Changes in the price of shares in the USA in the years 1925–33

Source B: A statement by a leading US economist in 1928, explaining the fears that some economists had about the dramatic rise in share prices

Sooner or later, a crash is coming, and it may be terrific, factories will be shut down, men will be thrown out of work and there will be a serious business depression.

Source C: A businessman warns in 1928 about the dangers of over-speculation

The number of inexperienced speculators is being increased by a great many men who have been attracted by newspaper stories. The stories tell of the big, easy profits to be made on the stock exchange. These amateurs have not learnt that markets sometimes panic and that there are large falls in prices. These suckers speculate on tips, on hunches. They buy or sell at the slightest notice.

Practice question

Study Sources B and C. Which of the sources is more useful to an historian studying the problems in the stock market in the late 1920s? *(For guidance, see pages 164–165.)*

ACTIVITIES

1. Study Figure 5.2. What does it tell you about share prices in the USA between 1925 and 1933?
2. How did the availability of easy credit contribute to the rise in share prices?

The Wall Street Crash

The boom of the 1920s ended abruptly and dramatically with the Wall Street Crash of October 1929.

Panic selling

When, in the autumn of 1929, some experts started to sell their shares heavily before their value fell even further, small investors panicked. They saw the fall in prices and rushed to sell their own shares – as can be seen in Figure 5.3. This led to a complete collapse of prices and thousands of investors lost millions of dollars.

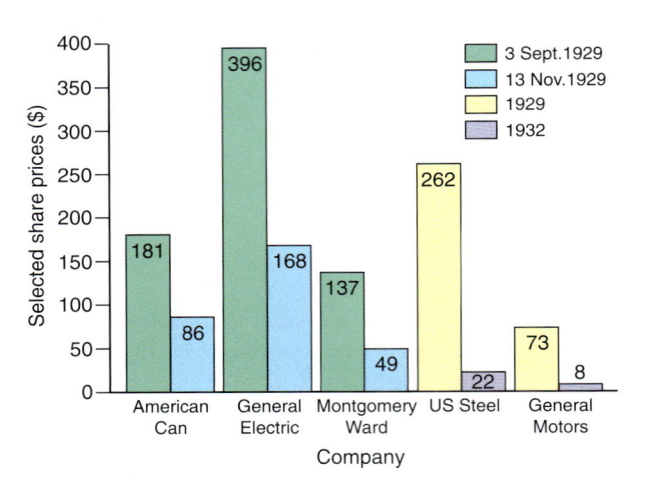

▲ Figure 5.3: Decline in share values between 1929 and 1932

The following headlines show the events of October 1929.

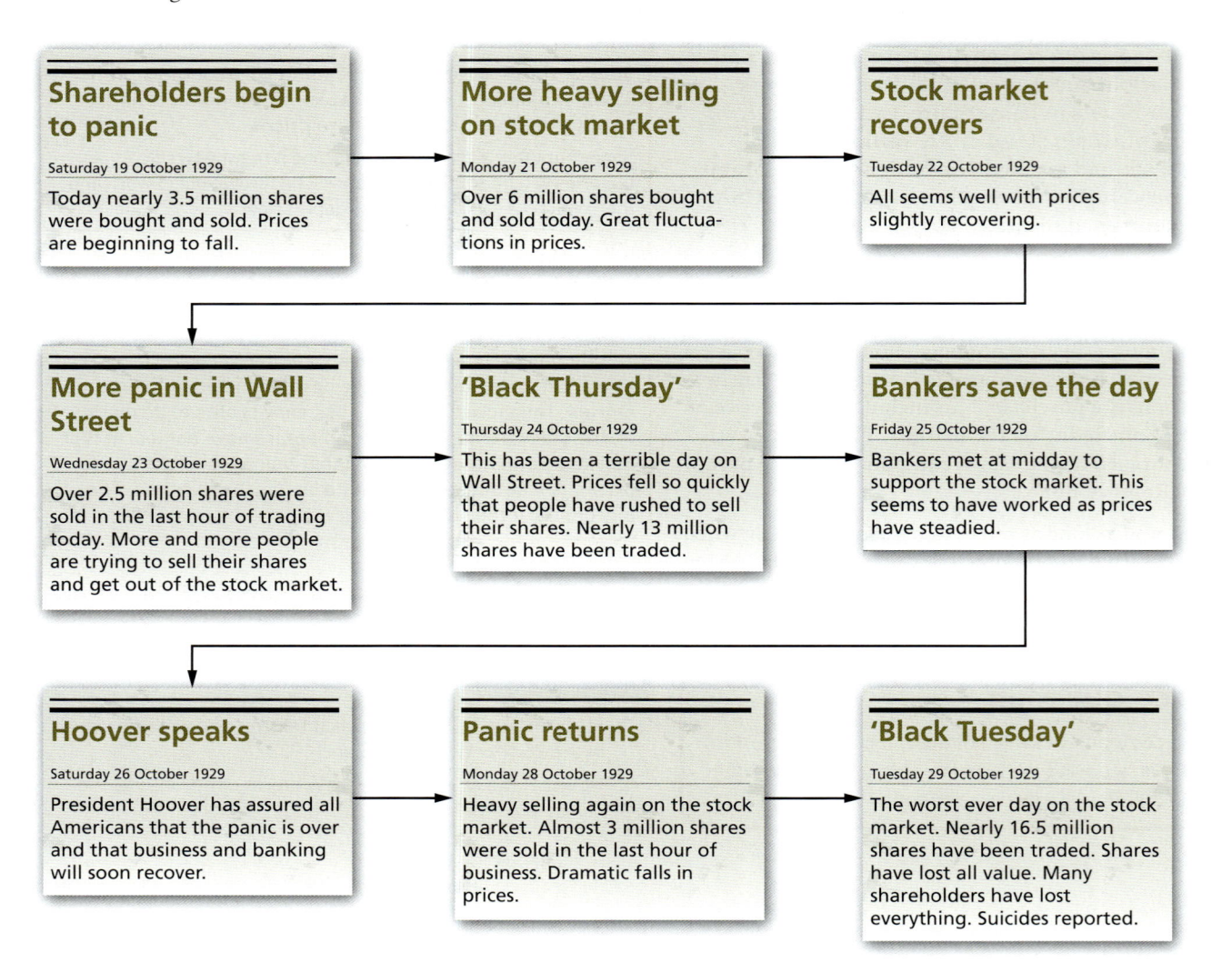

Shareholders begin to panic
Saturday 19 October 1929
Today nearly 3.5 million shares were bought and sold. Prices are beginning to fall.

More heavy selling on stock market
Monday 21 October 1929
Over 6 million shares bought and sold today. Great fluctuations in prices.

Stock market recovers
Tuesday 22 October 1929
All seems well with prices slightly recovering.

More panic in Wall Street
Wednesday 23 October 1929
Over 2.5 million shares were sold in the last hour of trading today. More and more people are trying to sell their shares and get out of the stock market.

'Black Thursday'
Thursday 24 October 1929
This has been a terrible day on Wall Street. Prices fell so quickly that people have rushed to sell their shares. Nearly 13 million shares have been traded.

Bankers save the day
Friday 25 October 1929
Bankers met at midday to support the stock market. This seems to have worked as prices have steadied.

Hoover speaks
Saturday 26 October 1929
President Hoover has assured all Americans that the panic is over and that business and banking will soon recover.

Panic returns
Monday 28 October 1929
Heavy selling again on the stock market. Almost 3 million shares were sold in the last hour of business. Dramatic falls in prices.

'Black Tuesday'
Tuesday 29 October 1929
The worst ever day on the stock market. Nearly 16.5 million shares have been traded. Shares have lost all value. Many shareholders have lost everything. Suicides reported.

5 The end of prosperity

Source D: Cecil Roberts wrote about the Wall Street Crash in *The Bright Twenties*, 1938

The stock market hysteria reached its peak in 1929. Everyone was playing the market … On my last day in New York, I went down to the barber. As he removed the sheet he said softly, 'Buy Standard Gas. I've doubled … It's good for another double.' As I walked upstairs, I reflected that if the hysteria had reached the barber level, something must soon happen.

▲ **Source E:** Depositors outside a bank in New Jersey, trying to get in to withdraw their deposits on *Black Tuesday*, 29 October 1929

ACTIVITIES

1. How useful are Sources D and E to an historian studying the reasons for the Wall Street Crash?
2. Explain why share prices in the USA fell rapidly during October 1929.
3. Study the newspaper headlines on page 138. Imagine you are a British radio reporter who witnessed the Wall Street Crash. Describe to your listeners the sequence of events from 19 to 29 October.

Practice question

Use Source E and your own knowledge to describe the events of Black Tuesday, 29 October 1929. *(For guidance, see pages 159–160.)*

139

The immediate effects of the Wall Street Crash

The impact of the Crash was quite spectacular. The stock market completely collapsed (see Sources F and G).

By the end of 1929 there were about 2.5 million unemployed in the USA. However, this amounted to only five per cent of the workforce, and some felt that the country would see out the crisis. But confidence had died, and those who had money were unwilling to spend. Unemployment began to gather pace as fewer and fewer consumer goods were purchased – the amount of goods sold in retail stores halved in the years 1929–33.

Suddenly the USA became a land of unemployment, tramps, bread queues and soup kitchens. Many people were evicted from their homes and lived on the streets – children included. It was the time of the **hobo** – thousands of men travelled the country hitching rides on railcars and freight wagons.

> **Source F:** *The New York Times*, 30 October 1929
>
> Stock prices virtually collapsed yesterday, swept downwards with gigantic losses in the most disastrous trading day in the stock market's history. Billions of dollars in market value were wiped out. The market on the rampage is no respecter of persons. It wasted fortune after fortune yesterday and financially crippled thousands of individuals in all parts of the world.

> **Source G:** American writer, Carl Sandburg, describes the collapse in share sales in *The People, Yes*, 1936
>
> Shares in a cigar company at the time of the crash were selling for $115. The market collapsed and the share dropped to $2 and the company president jumped from his Wall Street office window.

The Depression

People were not buying goods and even the rich began to economise. Employers began to lay off employees. Servants were sacked and those who were able to find jobs worked for lower wages than they had before. The economy was spiralling downwards.

The Depression was not caused by the Crash. The issues with the economy in the 1920s are vital in understanding what was wrong with the US at that time – look once more at pages 135–136. However, the Crash did speed up the approach of the Depression, and its effects were catastrophic for the country and the people during the next decade.

- Many stockbrokers were unable to repay their debts to the banks – many banks went bust.
- Thousands of people who had saved in banks were bankrupted.
- Workforces were laid off.
- Credit collapsed and loans were taken in.
- Those banks that survived were unwilling to make further loans – the time of speculation and risk-taking was over.

Farmers were hit terribly, and when they demonstrated in towns they carried placards attacking the president. One slogan became extremely popular: 'In Hoover we trusted, now we are busted.'

▲ **Source H:** A stockbroker trying to sell his car in late October 1929 following the events of the Wall Street Crash.

> **Source I:** From the memoirs of a young British journalist, Alistair Cooke, who had been sent to America in the late 1920s. They were published in his book *Letters from America* (1951)
>
> Only the poor had nothing to lose. When steel stocks went from 90 to 12 the automobile companies simply let half their workers go. There were skyscrapers finished who had no tenants. There were truckers and nothing to truck, crops that went unharvested, milk that went undelivered to people who couldn't afford it. I couldn't go out in the evening without being stopped by nicely dressed men who had told their wives they were looking for night work. So they were – they were out on the streets cadging dimes and quarters.

6 Popular entertainment

DUKE ELLINGTON 1899–1974

He was born in Washington DC in 1899 and became a composer and pianist. In the 1920s, he moved to New York, where he assembled a ten-piece band. He became popular because of recordings such as 'Choo Choo' and 'Chocolate Kiddies'.

LOUIS ARMSTRONG 1901–71

He was born in New Orleans in 1901 and became famous as a trumpeter there. In 1922, he moved to Chicago, known as the jazz capital of the USA. By 1925, he had his own band and was known nationwide. Some of his famous recordings included 'Ain't Misbehavin', and 'Tiger Rag'.

ACTIVITIES

1. Study Source H. What does it tell you about how some Americans viewed the impact of jazz?
2. Explain why jazz music became so popular in America during the 1920s.

Practice questions

1. Use Source I and your own knowledge to describe jazz music in the 1920s. *(For guidance, see pages 159–160.)*
2. Study Sources F and G. Which of the sources is more useful to an historian studying the impact of jazz on American society? *(For guidance, see pages 164–165.)*

▲ **Source I:** King Oliver and his Creole Jazz Band, Chicago, 1922. Louis Armstrong is the musician in the middle, at the back

The impact of the radio and gramophone

The radio had a massive influence on many Americans. The first radio station, Station KDKA, began in 1920 and by 1930 there were more than 600 radio stations in the USA and 40 per cent of US homes had a radio set. Many families bought radios on weekly instalments and mass production helped to lower the cost of buying them.

Radio enabled people to listen to sporting events, music, for example, jazz, as well as advertisements. News, sport and entertainment were easily relayed into millions of homes. The first national radio network, the National Broadcasting Company (NBC), was set up in 1926, followed a year later by the Columbia Broadcasting System (CBS). Indeed, radio became the main source of family entertainment. It created sporting heroes such as the boxer, Jack Dempsey, and the baseball player, Babe Ruth. It made events accessible to many people who could not afford to attend. As radio reached more than 50 million people by the end of the 1920s, there was a dramatic increase in political and social awareness among the population at large, for people no longer had to be literate to follow the news.

> **ACTIVITY**
>
> Study Source J. What impact did the radio have on popular entertainment during the 1920s?

> **Practice question**
>
> Use Source K and your own knowledge to describe the use of the radio as a popular form of entertainment in the 1920s. *(For guidance, see pages 159–160.)*

Source J: From a US newspaper article in 1929

From the feeble wireless telegraph service in 1920, radio has grown swiftly into the billion dollar industry it is today. Advertising has made broadcasting an industry. The broadcasters discovered they could boost the car industry or the ginger beer industry. And then time on the air becomes something that people want to buy.

The **gramophone** industry grew rapidly after 1900, peaking in 1921 with sales of $106 million. However, by 1922, radio had destroyed the market with the free music it offered over the airwaves. Sales fell throughout the entire decade, and when the stock market crashed in 1929, most of the smaller companies either went out of business or were bought by larger companies.

▲ **Source K:** A flapper wearing headphones to listen to the radio in the mid-1920s

6 Popular entertainment

Dancing

One of the biggest changes in popular culture during this period was in dancing. Dances before the First World War were slow and rather formal, but there was a more carefree approach in the 1920s. One of the most well-known dances of the time was the Charleston, which had a breath-taking pace and sudden shifting rhythms. Other popular dances were the black bottom (see Source M), the vampire, shimmy, turkey trot, buzzard lope, chicken scratch, monkey glide and the bunny hug. The Charleston and other modern dances shocked the older generation and many people considered them immoral and scandalous (see Source L).

> **Source L:** Reverend Burke Culpepper, a Fundamentalist preacher, delivering a sermon at Mount Vernon Methodist Episcopal Church, 1925
>
> Dancing is a divorce feeder. It is heathen, animalistic and damnable. It degrades womanhood and manhood. Now is the time to say plainly that it is one of the most pernicious of all modern customs.

Dance marathons

As the new jazz dances swept the country, dance marathons became popular. These were contests of self-endurance and human record setting, with dances continuing non-stop until one couple remained standing to claim the prize money. The participants hoped to win not only some money but achieve fame, even if it was for a short time. The craze began in 1923 when 32-year-old Alma Cummings danced non-stop for 27 hours. She wore out six different partners and acquired some national fame for the achievement. It was soon realised that money could be made from these marathons, both for participants and for the promoters. The competitions would sometimes last for weeks and special rules were drawn up, for example specifying the rest periods, changing clothes, having a massage and so on. There was no demand that people actually had to dance; provided the competitors moved the judges were satisfied.

Many dance competitors thought of themselves as show business stars and some hoped to break into films. However, the only dancers who hit the big time were June Havoc and Red Skelton.

▲ **Source M:** Joan crawford dances the black bottom in sequence

▲ **Source N:** A couple participating in a dance marathon, 1925

ACTIVITIES

1. What does Source M suggest about the new styles of dance in the 1920s?
2. Explain why dance marathons became popular during the 1920s.
3. How useful is Source L to an historian studying the reasons why some American disliked the new jazz culture?

The speakeasy culture

A key feature of the Prohibition era was the development of the speakeasy culture. The introduction of Prohibition in 1920 resulted in an increase in drinking clubs, commonly referred to as speakeasies. The entertainment in the speakeasies was often provided by groups of black Americans playing jazz. The speakeasies allowed whites and blacks to mingle socially for the first time and they drew young audiences from all social classes. Young people were attracted to both the music and the increasingly suggestive jazz dances. The prices in the speakeasies where alcohol was consumed ensured the clientele was mainly middle class. Both the mixing of the races and the widespread belief that jazz incited sexual activity caused large numbers of people to oppose jazz whenever possible.

Gang bosses opened fancy clubs with dancers and the hottest bands as the cabaret. At Small's Paradise in Harlem, New York, waiters danced the Charleston, carrying trays loaded down with cocktails. Popular stars like Fred and Adele Astaire entertained at The Trocadero, and at the Cotton Club Duke Ellington led the house band and tap dancer Bojangles Robinson and jazz singer Ethel Waters were the other main attractions.

Source O: F Scott Fitzgerald, a contemporary novelist, describes changes in cultural activity in the early 1920s in *Tales of the Jazz Age* (1922)

The parties were bigger – the pace was faster – the shows were broader, the buildings were higher, the morals were looser and the liquor was cheaper.

ACTIVITY

Study Sources O and P. What do they tell us about the speakeasy culture of the 1920s?

Practice question

Was the radio the most important change in popular entertainment in the USA during the 1920s? Use your own knowledge and understanding of the issue to support your answer. *(For guidance, see pages 166–167.)*

▲ **Source P:** Popular entertainment in a speakeasy in the late 1920s

7 The role of women

During the early twentieth century, attitudes towards the role and status of women underwent substantial change. Before the First World War few women had careers. Their lifestyle was restricted by social convention and middle and upper class ladies led secluded lives. The First World War gave women the opportunity to enter the workplace and they played an important role in helping the US war effort in the years 1917–18. In 1920, after a long campaign, they were granted the right to vote in the USA. For some women, the 1920s was a period of great change, especially in their social position and appearance. They embraced the new fashions and new social life, and adopted a more independent lifestyle. These new women were known as flappers. For many women, however, due to their economic circumstances, religious or other beliefs, there was little change in their status or employment opportunities.

The role of women in the pre-war years

Political role
Women were not allowed to play a part in politics. They did not have the vote.

Social role
It was thought to be unladylike for a woman to smoke or drink in public. A woman would be accompanied by a chaperone if she went out during the day or evening. Divorce and sex before marriage were rare.

Employment opportunities
These were limited and most middle- and upper-class women did not go out to work as this interfered with their domestic role as a mother and housewife. Most working women were in low-paid jobs such as cleaning, dress-making and secretarial work.

Appearance
Women were expected to wear tight-waisted, ankle-length dresses, have long hair, which was tied back, and not wear make-up.

Practice question
Describe the position of women in the USA in the early twentieth century. *(For guidance, see page 161.)*

The impact of the First World War

The American entry into the First World War in 1917 provided greater opportunities for women:

- Around 2.8 million men had been drafted into the armed forces by the end of the war and more than a million women helped with the war effort.
- Approximately 90,000 women served in the US armed forces in Europe. The Navy and Marine Corps enlisted women as clerks, radio electricians, chemists, accountants and nurses. Others joined the Young Women's and Young Men's Christian Associations, the American Red Cross and the Salvation Army. The army, unlike its sister services, was more conservative in the jobs it permitted women to fill its ranks, enlisting more than 21,000 as clerks, fingerprint experts, journalists and translators.
- Women also worked in jobs traditionally done by men, such as heavy industry, engineering works and transport.

The war proved women could do the jobs just as well as men and encouraged greater freedom, especially in social habits such as smoking and drinking in public, and going out un-chaperoned. Their participation also made a powerful argument for women being given the right to vote.

ACTIVITY

How important was the First World War in helping to change the position of women in American society?

Practice question

Use Source A and your own knowledge to describe the part played by women in the war effort. *(For guidance, see pages 159–160.)*

▲ **Source A:** Women making machine gun parts in a factory in New Haven, Connecticut in 1918

Changing political attitudes

The 1920s saw a series of changes to the political and economic position of women.

Securing the right to vote

Women's suffrage groups such as the North American Women Suffrage Association (formed in 1890) and the Congressional Union for Women's Suffrage (formed in 1913) had been campaigning for the vote but had been unsuccessful in persuading many politicians to back their cause. The turning point for women's suffrage came as a result of the impact of the First World War. The contribution of women to the war effort made their demands for political equality hard to resist. As a result the 19th Amendment became law in 1920, granting women the right to vote. This gave them greater political power and encouraged some to campaign for further change.

Advances in politics

After securing the vote in 1920 a few women did make progress in gaining political power. For example, in 1924, Nellie Tayloe Ross of Wyoming became the first woman to be elected governor of a state. Two years later, Bertha Knight Landes became the first female mayor of an American city, Seattle.

However, these were the exceptions and women made little progress in politics itself. Political parties wanted their vote but did not see them as realistic candidates for political office. By 1920, there were still only a handful of female politicians. Most women, in any case, had little interest in politics. The **Women's Movement** failed in its attempt to get the Equal Rights Amendment Act passed, which would have given them equality in law with men.

> **ACTIVITY**
>
> How successful were women in making political progress during the 1920s?

> **Practice question**
>
> Use Source B and your own knowledge to describe the political progress made by women by 1920. *(For guidance, see pages 159–160.)*

◀ Source B: Suffragettes marching in a victory parade in New York following the passing of the 19th Amendment in 1920

The influence of jazz culture

During the 1920s younger middle- and upper-class women began to lead a more liberal lifestyle. They were influenced by the newly emerging jazz culture. The 'Jazz Age' brought changes in entertainment and leisure. The 1920s was styled the 'age of the flapper' as many new liberalised women went to the jazz clubs, dance halls and speakeasies.

Jazz music and the culture that went with it provided some women with an opportunity to break free from the norm and rebel. Jazz clubs, speakeasies and dance halls allowed women to escape from their traditional roles as daughters and mothers. Within these places women were also allowed greater freedom to express themselves in their language, clothing and behaviour.

Jazz culture also provided new jobs for women during the 1920s. Jazz venues were encouraged to employ flappers so that the establishments would appeal to the new youth culture of the 1920s. Furthermore, women like Lil Hardin and Bessie Smith paved the way for women to pursue careers in the popular performing arts. Women also found new employment in the advertising, cosmetic, and clothing industries, all of which were related to the jazz culture of the time.

Consumer goods, such as dancing garments, radios and cosmetics, revolved around jazz culture and advertising for these products targeted this new consumer group. For example, while older advertisements may have portrayed women fully clothed and accompanied by a man new advertising included images of the new liberalised and independent women, complete with short hair and fashionable clothes.

Not all American women, however, were able to live this kind of life. Some rejected the lifestyle because of their religious or social beliefs, condemning such women for being too immoral and too sexual. Others were forced to continue with their traditional role of being a housewife and mother because they lacked the economic means to afford the new clothes, fashions and nightlife culture. Most American women concentrated on making ends meet or setting aside money to purchase the new gadgets that offered some release from household drudgery.

> **Practice question**
>
> What was the purpose of Source C? *(For guidance, see pages 162–163.)*

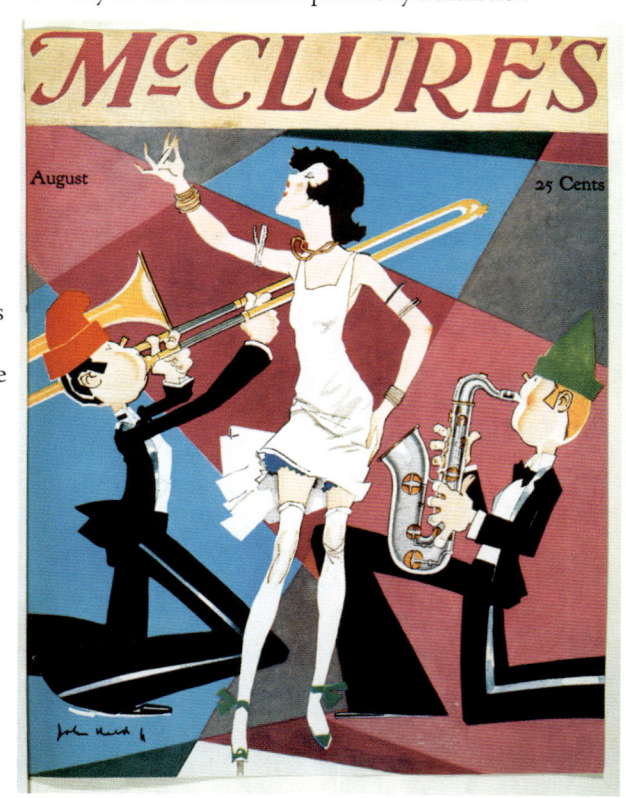

▲ **Source C:** The cover of a fashionable American magazine from 1925 showing the new jazz culture

The flapper lifestyle and feminism

The greatest change in the position of females was experienced by women known as the flappers. In the 1920s, a number of women, generally from middle- and upper-class families living in the northern states, decided to challenge the traditional attitudes towards women. They became known as the flappers. Their aim was to become more independent in their social life and to take a freer approach to their behaviour and appearance. Flappers celebrated their sexuality and independence, went out with their boyfriends, drank bootleg liquor, smoked in public and drove cars and motorbikes.

> **Source D:** A view of flappers from the *New York Times*, 1922
>
> A flapper is shameless, selfish and honest but at the same time she thinks of these things as good. Why not? She takes a man's point of view as her mother never could. When she loses she is not afraid to admit defeat, whether it be a lover or $20 at an auction. She will never make you a husband or knit you a necktie, but she'll drive you from the station on hot summer nights in her own sports car. She'll put on trousers and go skiing with you or, if it happens to be summertime, go swimming.

> **Source E:** From a letter written by a feminist to the *Daily Illini* newspaper in 1922
>
> The word 'flapper' to us means not a female that smokes, swears and kisses her gentlemen friends goodnight, although there is no harm in any of that. We think of the flapper as the independent young woman who feels like punching someone when called the 'weaker sex', who resents being put on a pedestal and who is responsible for the advancement of women's condition in the world.

In the years after 1900 there were a number of women's associations involved in a variety of campaigns. Some campaigned for greater employment opportunities and equal pay. Others were more concerned with improved political rights, especially the vote. This feminist movement achieved success when, in 1920, women were allowed to vote for the first time in presidential elections. However, during the 1920s, in spite of or even because of, the flapper image, the feminist movement weakened. The majority of women were uninterested in politics.

Flapper icons and role models

Actress Joan Crawford was the most famous flapper of them all. She kissed, drank, smoked and danced the Charleston in films such as *Our Modern Maidens* (1929). Girls loved it and tried to copy her. The silent film star Louise Brooks was another flapper icon. Her first on-screen role as a flapper was in the 1926 film *A Social Celebrity*. Brooks would also play flapper-like characters in *Love 'Em and Leave 'Em* (1926) and *Rolled Stockings* (1927). Other popular flappers included Colleen Moore and Clara Bow, the so-called 'It Girl' due to her flapper role in the film *It* (1927) (see page 144).

ACTIVITIES

1. How did the lives of some women change during the 1920s?
2. Explain why some women were unable to make changes to their lifestyle.
3. Working in pairs, make a copy of the set of scales. Using evidence from pages 151–154:
   - ☐ one person should write examples of progress on the left-hand side of the scale
   - ☐ the other should write examples of lack of progress on right-hand side of the scale.

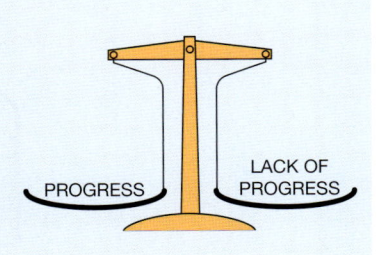

> **Source F:** F. Scott Fitzgerald was a famous American author who wrote about the roaring twenties. In 1920 he married Zelda Zayre, who was a typical flapper
>
> Flirting, kissing, viewing life lightly, saying damn without a blush, playing along the danger line in an immature way – a sort of mental baby vamp.

New fashions

Flappers adopted the new fashion of short skirts (as high as just below the knee) and straight sleeveless dresses. They cut their hair short and wore make-up and perfume. Flappers also wore revealing swimming costumes on public beaches.

- They cut their hair short and wore make-up.
- They wore short skirts and very bright clothes.
- They smoked and drank in public.
- They went out to speakeasies and to the cinema without a chaperone.
- They openly danced with men in public, especially the new craze, the Charleston, and listened to controversial new music known as jazz.
- They drove cars, and even motorbikes.
- They wore very revealing swimming costumes on public beaches.

▲ Figure 7.1: Flappers

Practice question

Study Sources D and E. Which of the sources is more useful to an historian studying attitudes towards flappers? *(For guidance, see pages 164–165.)*

ACTIVITIES

1. Explain why flappers were viewed as a threat to the traditional lifestyle of women.
2. Use Figure 7.1 and your own knowledge to write a description of a typical flapper of the 1920s.

Opposition to the flapper lifestyle

In some respects the flapper lifestyle did little to further the cause of women's rights in the 1920s. Flappers were seen as too extreme by many traditional groups, especially in rural areas, and met with strong disapproval from religious societies. Many of the older generation criticised the lifestyle of the flappers and formed Anti-Flirt Leagues.

Some flappers deliberately flouted the law and were arrested, for example, for wearing revealing clothing such as banned swimsuits (see Source I). Others saw the flappers as simply pleasure-seeking women with few other attributes. While some strongly objected to the flapper lifestyle, other women were sympathetic but lacked the financial means or the opportunity to adopt the new fashions or to attend the new social events.

> **Source G:** An English journalist writing about flappers in the USA in 1921
>
> Think of the modern young American girl of this great country. Do they ever think? Do they ever ask whence they have come? It would seem not. Their aim appears to be to attract men and to secure money. What can a man with a mind find to hold him in one of these lovely, brainless, cigarette-smoking creatures of undisciplined sex whom he meets continually?

> **Source H:** An article called 'Flapper Jane' from a fashionable US magazine, 1925
>
> Jane's a flapper. Let us take a look at the young person as she strolls across the lawn of her parents' suburban home, having just put the car away after driving sixty miles in two hours. She is, for one thing, a pretty girl. Beauty is the fashion in 1925. She is frankly, heavily made up with poisonously scarlet lips and richly ringed eyes. As for her clothes, Jane isn't wearing much this summer. Her dress is brief. It is cut low. The skirt comes just below the knees. The bra has been abandoned since 1924.

▲ **Source I:** A group of flappers in Chicago being arrested for wearing banned one-piece bathing suits, which were seen as too figure-hugging

ACTIVITIES

1. Explain why some people opposed the flappers.
2. What does Source I tell you about the attitudes some authorities adopted towards flapper?
3. Study all the sources on pages 155–157 and copy and complete the following table. An example has been done for you.

Source	Positive features of flappers	Negative features
E		Pleasure seeking

Practice questions

1. Study Sources G and H. Which of the sources is more useful to an historian studying the reasons why some Americans opposed the flapper lifestyle? (For guidance, see pages 164–165.)
2. Was the granting of the vote the most important change in the lifestyle and status of women during this period? Use your own knowledge and understanding of the issue to support your answer. (For guidance, see pages 166–167.)

WJEC examination guidance

This section will give you step-by-step guidance on how best to approach and answer the types of questions that you will face in the exam. Below is model exam paper with a set of exam-style questions (without the sources).

Unit two: studies in depth

> In Question 1 you have to analyse an historical source and demonstrate your knowledge and understanding of the period by describing its key features in context.

> In Question 2 you have to demonstrate your own knowledge and understanding of a key feature. You should aim to include specific factual detail.

> In Question 3 you have to demonstrate knowledge and understanding through analysing and evaluating an historical source in order to explain its purpose (why it was produced).

> In Question 4 you have to demonstrate knowledge and understanding in order to provide a judgement about the usefulness of two sources to an historian, having analysed and evaluated the content and authorship of each source before reaching a judgement.

> In Question 5 you need to use your own knowledge to debate an issue, looking at both sides of the argument. You should provide a reasoned judgement upon the set question.

History with a European/World focus
2B: The USA: A Nation of Contrasts, 1910–29
Time allowed: 1 hour

1. This question is about religion and race in the USA.
   Study the source below and then answer the question that follows. Use Source A and your own knowledge to describe the activities of the KKK.
   [6 marks]

2. This question is about the economic boom.
   Describe how electrification contributed to the booming economy of the 1920s.
   [8 marks]

3. This question is about popular entertainment.
   What was the purpose of Source B? Use details from Source B and your own knowledge and understanding of the historical context to answer the question.
   [8 marks]

4. This question is about immigration in the USA.
   Study the sources and then answer the question that follows.
   Which of the sources is more useful to an historian studying the trial of Sacco and Vanzetti? You should refer to both sources in your answer and use your knowledge and understanding of this historical context.
   [12 marks]

5. This question is about the end of prosperity in the 1920s.
   Was the panic selling of shares the main cause of the Wall Street Crash in October 1929?
   [16 marks]
   Use your own knowledge and understanding of the issue to support your answer.
   Marks for spelling, punctuation and the accurate use of grammar and specialist language are allocated to this question.
   [3 marks]

Total marks for the paper: 53

WJEC Examination Guidance

Examination Guidance for Question 1

This section provides guidance on how to analyse an historical source and demonstrate your knowledge and understanding of the period by describing its key features in context. Look at the following question:

> Use Source A and your own knowledge to describe the treatment of black Americans living in the southern states.

▲ **Source A:** A segregated drinking fountain. These were common across the southern states of America

How to answer

1. Underline the key words in the question. This will enable you to focus on what the examiner wants you to write about.
2. Describe what you can see or read in the source, remembering to make use of the information provided in the caption of a visual source.
3. Link this information to your knowledge of this period.
4. Aim to make at least two developed points.

159

Example answer

Step One: Describe what you can see or read in the source, remembering to make use of the information provided in the caption.

> The photograph provides an example of how black Americans living in the southern states were forced to accept the Jim Crow laws of segregation. The photograph shows a black American drinking from a segregated water fountain. The facility for coloured Americans is of poor quality in comparison to that available for White Americans, and it shows how black Americans were treated as second class citizens under the Jim Crow laws.

Step Two: Use your knowledge of this topic to expand what you have said about the source, including specific historical detail if possible, to provide context.

> The caption says that this segregation was common across the southern states. It was evident in all areas of everyday life. Segregation existed on public transport, in hospitals, restaurants, cinemas, theatres, swimming pools and schools. It meant that black Americans experienced poorer services and were forced to live in the poorest areas. They were forced to work in the lowest paid jobs and they received little legal protection. Through segregation white Americans living in the south were able to control the lives of black Americans.

> Now try the following question:
>
> Use Source B and your own knowledge to describe the impact of the Wall Street Crash.

Source B: A stockbroker trying to sell his car in late October 1929 following the events of the Wall Street Crash

Examination Guidance for Question 2

This section provides guidance on how to answer a 'describe' question which requires you to demonstrate specific knowledge and understanding of a key feature. Look at the following question:

> Describe what happened during the Wall Street Crash of October 1929.

How to answer

1. Make sure you only include information that is directly relevant.
2. It is good practice to start your answer using the words from the question. For example: 'The Wall Street Crash was the result of …'
3. Try to include specific factual details such as dates, events, names of key people.
4. Aim to cover a number of key points in some detail.

Example answer

> The Wall Street Crash was the direct result of the panic selling of shares following over-speculation on the US stock market. Share prices had continued to rise during 1929 to unrealistic highs. Many ordinary Americans had jumped onto the band wagon and bought shares, often borrowing money to do so. They were dangerously exposed to any sharp fall in share prices. Warning bells began to ring on 19 October when several big investors sold large quantities of shares. This caused prices to fall but many thought it was just a temporary fall and they would soon rise again.

Step One: Introduce the topic, maintaining a clear focus on what the question is asking.

> However, prices continued to fall and on 24 October, nicknamed 'Black Thursday', over 12 million shares were sold. Panic now set in and many nervous investors attempted to sell their shares. This caused prices to fall even lower. Everybody wanted to sell and very few investors wanted to buy. Prices continued to slide downwards. The worst day of trading on the stock market occurred on 'Black Tuesday', 29 October, when 16 million shares were sold.

Step Two: Provide specific factual detail, covering a range of key points.

> By the end of the month, the US stock market had crashed and shares were worth only a fraction of they had been a few months earlier. There was a loss of confidence in the financial sector causing many banks to go bust. Millions of Americans had lost their money as their shares were now worthless. Some investors committed suicide as they felt their world had come to end as they had lost everything. The Crash was to have long-term economic consequences for America.

Step Three: Aim to provide good context to the event you are describing.

> Now try the following question:
>
> Describe how immigration into the USA was limited after the First World War.

WJEC GCSE History: Germany in Transition, 1919–39 and the USA: A Nation of Contrasts, 1910–29

Examination Guidance for Question 3

This section provides guidance on how to analyse and evaluate an historical source in order to explain its purpose. Look at the following question:

> What was the purpose of Source A? Use details from Source A and your own knowledge and understanding of the historical context to answer the question.

▲ **Source A:** An advertisement from 1927 for the film *The Jazz Singer*. It was the first full-length 'talkie' film

How to answer

1 You need to spell out why this source was produced.
2 Use your knowledge of this topic area when considering the content of the source and what it shows.
3 Make use of the information provided in the caption/attribution of the source. This can supply important information such as publication date, the name of the newspaper, book or magazine.
4 Use this information to help identify motive.
   ■ Who was the intended audience?
   ■ What did the source aim to do?

WJEC Examination Guidance

Example answer

The advertisement dates from 1927 and refers to the showing of a film called *The Jazz Singer*, which starred Al Jolson. This film made history because it was the first 'talking' picture and Al Jolson became the first actor to speak on film. Up to this time all films had been silent ones. This was the start of a new era in cinema history. The purpose of the poster was to advertise this new type of film technology.

Step One: Pick out key details from the caption and from what you can see/read in the source to make a judgement on its purpose – when and why was the source produced?

The cinema had developed during the 1920s into one of the most popular forms of entertainment in America, with a large percentage of the population making regular visits. *The Jazz Singer* contained sound which in the poster is referred to as 'Vitaphone'. This allowed the audience to hear what the actors were saying and this helped to make the cinema even more popular in the late 1920s. The film company, Warner Brothers, are advertising this new invention and want to attract vast audiences. They are showing the film twice daily, with an extra matinee on a Sunday. This highlights the growing popularity of the cinema at this time.

Step Two: Use your knowledge of this topic area to develop the main message of the source. Pick out key details and link them to what was happening at the time to provide context.

This new technology of using 'Vitaphone' marked the end of the silent era and the birth of the 'talkie' film industry. Many of the stars of the silent era did not survive in talking pictures and new film stars emerged. The advertisement signalled a key change in the history of the cinema. It was produced to advertise the new development of sound in films. Its key motive was commercial, to attract people to watch the film. It helped to make the cinema even more popular as a form of entertainment.

Step Three: Remember to address the key issue – suggest reasons why the source was produced at that time.

Now try the following question:

What was the purpose of Source B? Use details from Source B and your own knowledge and understanding of the historical context to answer the question.

◀ **Source B:** A cartoon which appeared in an American newspaper in 1922 showing the Teapot Dome Scandal. One of the figures running away is Albert Fall

163

WJEC GCSE History: Germany in Transition, 1919–39 and the USA: A Nation of Contrasts, 1910–29

Examination Guidance for Question 4

This section provides guidance on how to provide a judgement about the usefulness of two sources to an historian, having analysed and evaluated the content and authorship of each source. Look at the following question:

> Which of the following sources is more useful to an historian studying the impact of Prohibition upon American life?

Source A: Part of a speech given by Pauline Sabin in 1929 in which she called for the repeal of Prohibition. Sabin founded the Women's Organisation for National Prohibition Reform in Chicago in 1929

Prohibition has led to more violation of and contempt for the law, to more hypocrisy among private citizens as well as police officers than any other thing in our national life. It is responsible for the greatest organised criminal class in the country. ... It is time to replace the present corruption, lawlessness and hypocrisy with honesty.

Source B: Part of an interview with a gangster about true-life American crime for a magazine article which was published shortly after Prohibition ended in 1933

We made our money by supplying a public demand. If I was supposed to have broken the law, my customers, who numbered hundreds of the best people in Chicago, were as guilty as I am. The only difference between me and them was that I sold and they bought. Many people called me a gangster and bootlegger. Others saw me as a businessman supplying their need.

How to answer

1. Underline key words in the question. This will enable you to focus on what the examiner wants you to write about.
2. In your answer you have to evaluate the usefulness of two sources to the historian studying the key issue named in the question.
3. For each source you must determine usefulness in terms of:
    - content value (what the source tells you about the key issue)
    - authorship (who said it and when)
    - the intended audience (why was the source produced and what was it purpose?)
    - the context (link the source content to the bigger picture of what was happening at that time).
4. Remember to provide a reasoned judgement on which source is the most useful and why.

Example answer

Step One: Provide an initial judgement, supported by contextual knowledge.

> Both sources are of varying usefulness to an historian studying the impact of Prohibition upon American life. One source outlines how Prohibition has been the direct cause of an increase in organised crime and lawlessness, while the other supports the breaking of Prohibition in order to provide a public service, providing alcohol to those who needed it.

Step Two: Evaluate the usefulness of Source A in terms of its content, authorship and context.

> Source A is useful because it clearly highlights the problems caused by Prohibition and the impact it had on American life. The author suggests the many people have violated the act, ordinary people as well as those in authority such as police officers. The breaking of the Prohibition laws was the primary cause of the increase in organised crime which resulted in the rise of powerful gangster gangs. These gangsters or bootleggers supplied the illegal alcohol to whoever wanted it, making large profits in the process. They protected their patch and this resulted in an increase in violence such as the St Valentine's Day massacre. They also bribed police officers, judges and city mayors like 'Big Bill' Thompson of Chicago, hence the reference made by the author to corruption and hypocrisy.

WJEC Examination Guidance

The author of Source A was Pauline Sabin who led a campaign to end Prohibition. She founded the Organization for National Prohibition Reform in Chicago in 1929, a city which was under the control of the gangster Al Capone. Sabin wished to justify why she wanted an end to Prohibition and in her speech she concentrated upon the negatives, and may well have exaggerated a little. She made very generalised points which were not backed up with specific details. However, the source is useful as it provides information about the arguments used by the anti-Prohibition movement to bring about reform.

Step Three: Provide a judgement on usefulness in terms of the accuracy of content and its purpose.

Source B is useful because it provides a very contrasting viewpoint. It is the view of a former gangster who was interviewed in the early 1930s, shortly after the ending of Prohibition. The gangster admits that he provided illegal alcohol to customers but he did not view this as breaking the law. He believed he was providing a much-needed service to the community. There was a demand for alcohol and he was supplying that demand. He was acting as a businessman not a bootlegger.

Step Four: Evaluate the usefulness of Source B in terms of its content, authorship and context.

This source is useful to the historian because although it is a very biased viewpoint, it does illustrate the age of Prohibition from the gangster point of view. However, the former gangster could be glamorising his past achievements to justify his breaking of the law.

Step Five: Provide a judgement on usefulness in terms of the accuracy of content and its purpose.

Both sources are useful to the historian. Source A contains a strong argument supporting the widely held belief that Prohibition had a very negative impact upon American life, being a direct cause of the rise of the gangsters and organised crime on a large scale. Source B provides a contrast, arguing that most people did not see the buying and selling of alcohol as a crime and they did not view the gangsters who supplied the alcohol as criminals. Both sources are useful in their own ways, as they provide contrasting views about the impact of Prohibition upon American lives.

Step Six: Provide an overall reasoned judgement about which source is the most useful.

Now try the following question:

Which of the following sources is more useful to an historian studying the trial of Sacco and Vanzetti?

Source C: A comment made against Judge Thayer who presided over the original Sacco and Vanzetti case. It was made in 1930 by Felix Frankfurter, a lawyer who campaigned for a retrial, and who wrote a book which criticised the original trial

I have known Judge Thayer all my life. I say that he is a narrow-minded man; he is an unintelligent man; he is full of prejudice; he is carried away by fear of Reds, a fear which has captured about ninety per cent of the American people.

Source D: Comments made by Bartolomeo Vanzetti as he and Nicola Sacco were led from court after having been found guilty of the murder of Fred Parmenter during a raid on a factory in Massachusetts in 1920

What I say is that I am innocent ... It is seven years that we are in jail. What we have suffered no human tongue can say, and yet you see me before you, not trembling, you see me looking in your eyes straight ... not ashamed or in fear ... We were tried in a time that has now passed into history. I mean by that, a time when there was hysteria of resentment and hate against the people of our principles, against the foreigner.

165

WJEC GCSE History: Germany in Transition, 1919–39 and the USA: A Nation of Contrasts, 1910–29

Examination Guidance for Question 5

This section provides guidance on how to debate an issue, looking at both sides of the argument, before providing a reasoned judgement upon the set question.

> Was the growth of the cinema the most important development in popular entertainment in America during this period? Use your own knowledge and understanding of the issue to support your answer.

How to answer

1. You need to develop a two-sided answer which has balance and good support.
2. Start by discussing the key issue identified in the question. Use your knowledge to explain why this factor is important.
3. You then need to consider the counter-argument. You need to cover a range of 'other factors'.
4. Support each factor with relevant factual detail.
5. Conclude your answer with a link back to the question and provide a judgement. How important is the factor identified in the question when compared against other factors?
6. Check over your answer for spelling, punctuation and grammar.

Example answer

Step One: Make sure your introduction demonstrates clear links to the question.

> The growth of the cinema played a significant part in the development of popular entertainment in America during this period. The silent cinema saw tremendous growth. In 1910, there were 8,000 cinemas and by 1930 this had grown to 303,000. They showed a variety of films covering many themes such as romance, westerns and slap-stick comedy. They provided an escape from ordinary life, where audiences could enjoy themselves in other worlds and situations. As entry prices were cheap most Americans were able to visit the cinema on a regular basis. A night in the cinema became a common social outing enjoyed by millions of Americans each week.

Step Two: Support your discussion of the key factor with relevant factual detail.

> As audience figures grew and more and more cinemas opened, there was a corresponding growth in film production companies like Warner Brothers, Paramount and Columbia. Movie stars began to attract followings of dedicated fans and stars such as Charlie Chaplin, Clara Bow, Mary Pickford and Rudolph Valentino became major celebrities. When Valentino died suddenly in 1926 over 100,000 fans lined the streets of New York to watch his funeral. Advances in technology helped to increase audience figures especially after the appearance of The Jazz Singer in 1927, the first talking picture. The cinema changed the social lives of millions of Americans and it became one of the most popular forms of entertainment.

Step Three: Begin the counter-argument using terms such as 'however' or 'one the other hand'. This makes it clear you are now looking at other factors.

> However, the cinema was not the only cultural and social development to affect America during this period. Another important development was the impact of jazz music. This was the music of black Americans, which developed in the Deep South and became popular during the 1920s. Jazz musicians like Louis Armstrong and Duke Ellington became household names as did singers such as Bessie Smith. Jazz bands toured the country playing to large audiences and selling records by the millions.

WJEC Examination Guidance

A close rival to the cinema as a popular form of entertainment was listening to the radio. Cheap radio sets allowed people to feel connected and to share experiences. It provided instant news and coverage of live events such as the music of jazz bands, sporting fixtures or messages from the president. It connected to audiences even in the remotest parts of the country. These isolated communities might not have a cinema but most homes did possess a radio. The radio therefore established itself during the 1920s as a popular source of entertainment.

Step Four: Support your discussion of other factors with relevant factual detail.

Another significant aspect of popular entertainment was the development of the speakeasy culture. Illegal drinking bars and clubs were to be found in most towns and cities. People visited them to buy illegal alcohol and to socialise. Clubs provided opportunities for dancing and with the development of jazz music new dances such as the Charleston and the Black Bottom became very popular. One craze of the 1920s was dance marathon competitions where couples competed to see who could stay dancing on the dance floor the longest.

Step Five: Aim to cover a range of factors, making sure you link them to the actual question. In this instance the other factors include references to the radio, jazz music, dance clubs and speakeasies.

During the 1920s, people had more leisure time and disposable income to engage in cultural and social events. They listened to the new jazz music on the radio and they went to nightclubs and dance halls. However, one of the greatest changes was due to the growth of the cinema. It was cheap entertainment enjoyed by millions of Americans, making it the most important development in popular entertainment during this period.

Step Six: Conclude your essay by providing a reasoned judgement – was the key factor identified in the question the most important factor or where other factors more important?

Step Seven: Read through your answer, checking for grammatical accuracy in terms of spelling, punctuation and grammar.

Now try the following question:

Were the activities of the KKK the worst examples of racial intolerance in the USA between 1910 and 1929?

Use your own knowledge and understanding of the issue to support your answer.

167

Glossary

Germany in Transition, 1919–1939

Adjutant An army officer who acts as an administrative assistant to a senior officer

Allied related to the Allied powers (Britain, France et al) of the First World War

Allies In the First World War, the powers that fought against Germany, Austria-Hungary, Turkey and Bulgaria

Annex Take over a territory or area

Anschluss Political and economic union of Germany and Austria

Anti-Semitism Hatred and persecution of the Jews

Appeasement Policy of making concessions to a potentially hostile nation in the hope of maintaining peace

Arbitration Accepting the decision of an agreed third party to settle a dispute

Armistice The ending of hostilities in a war

Aryan Nazi term for a non-Jewish German, someone of supposedly 'pure' German stock

Blitzkrieg 'Lightening war' – the new method used by the German armed forces in 1939

Bolshevik Revolution A revolution in Russia in 1917–18 that overthrew the Czar and brought the Bolsheviks to power

Bolsheviks Members of the Russian Social Democrat party, who followed Lenin and carried out a communist revolution in October 1917

Bolshevism The theory developed by the Bolsheviks between 1903 and 1917 with a view to seizing state power and establishing a dictatorship of the proletariat

Bund Deutscher Mädel League of German Girls, was the girls' wing of the Nazi Party youth movement

Censorship Controlling what speech or information is produced, and suppressing anything considered to be against the state

Centre Party (ZP) Catholic party occupying the middle ground in political views

Coalition government A government of two or more political parties

Communism A theory that society should be classless, private property abolished, and land and business owned collectively

Communists Followers of the communist ideas of Karl Marx, who believed, for example, that the state should own the means of production and distribution

Communist Party (KPD) The German Communist Party, following the ideas of Karl Marx

Concordat Agreement Agreement with the Roman Catholic Church

Conscription Compulsory military service for a certain period of time

Constituent Assembly A group of representatives elected to set up a new constitution

Dawes Plan Introduced in 1924 to reduce Germany's annual reparation payments

Democracy A system of government by the whole population or all the eligible members of a state, typically through elected representatives

Depression A period of extended and severe decline in a nation's economy, marked by low production and high unemployment

Dolchstoss The 'stab in the back' theory

DNVP Deutschnationale Volkspartei (see Nationalist Party)

Enabling Act The Act that gave Hitler the power to rule for four years without consulting the Reichstag

Enmities Hatreds

Führer German word for leader

German Faith Movement (*Deutsche Glaubensbewegung*) A religious movement in Nazi Germany that promoted Germanic paganism and Nazi ideas

Gestapo (*Geheime Staatspolizei* – '*Secret State Police*') Official secret police of the Nazi regime

Ghettos A densely populated area of a city inhabited by a particular ethnic group, such as Jews

Gleichschaltung The process of achieving rigid and total co-ordination and uniformity in politics, culture and communication by forcibly repressing or eliminating independence and freedom of thought, action or expression

Great Depression Slump in the economy in the 1930s which led to high unemployment

Great Power A nation that has exceptional political influence, resources and military strength

Hitler Youth (*HitlerJugend*) The organisation set up for the young in Germany to convert them to Nazi ideas and was eventually compulsory

Hyperinflation Extremely high inflation, where the value of money plummets and becomes almost worthless

Glossary

Industrialists People who own and/or run an industry or factory

Kaiser The German emperor

Kristallnacht 'Night of Broken Glass', when the windows of Jewish premises were smashed

League of Nations The international body established after the First World War in order to maintain peace

Lebensraum Living space. Hitler's desire to expand eastwards for living space for the German people

Left-wing Of politicians and parties that favour socialism

Nationalist Party Shortened form of the German National People's Party (DNVP)

Nationalists People who have a passionate devotion to their country

NSDAP The Nazi Party

Passive resistance Opposition to a government, invading power, etc., without using violence

Plebiscite Direct vote of the electorate on an important public issue

Polish Corridor The strip of German land that gave Poland access to the Baltic Sea

Proportional representation The number of votes won in an election determined the number of seats in the Reichstag

Putsch Attempted takeover of the government

RAD (*Reichsarbeitsdienst*) The National Labour Service Corps

Real wages Wages evaluated with reference to their purchasing power rather than to the money actually paid

Reich In German, this has many meanings – state, kingdom, empire. When used by the Nazis it tended to mean 'empire' or 'Germany'

Reichsbank German National Bank

Reparations War damages to be paid by Germany

Republic A state in which the government is carried out by the people or their elected representatives

Right wing The part of a political group that consists of people who support conservative or traditional ideas and policies and oppose social democracy

Self-determination The principle of nation states ruling themselves

Socialists Those who believe in state ownership

Soviet Union Also known as the Union of Soviet Socialist Republic (USSR) dominated by Russia

SD (*Sicherheitsdienst*) 'Security Service' – the intelligence agency of the Nazis

SS (*Schutzstaffel*) Originally Hitler's private bodyguard, but eventually grew to have very wide ranging powers

Sweated trades Jobs involving long hours in poor working conditions

Trade unions Organisations set up to protect and improve the rights of workers

Trade unionists Members of a trade union

Usury Money lending at very high rates, loan-sharking

Volksgemeinschaft The people's community. This was the Nazi idea of a community based upon the German race.

The USA: A Nation of Contrasts, 1910–29

Anarchism Belief in removing all forms of government

Anti-Saloon League An organisation founded in 1895 which campaigned for Prohibition

'Back to normalcy' Warren Harding's slogan promising a return to the more carefree days of 1917 – before the USA entered the First World War

Bible Belt Area of southern USA where Christian belief is strong

Black Power Movement Movement in support of improved rights for black Americans, which was prepared to use more violent methods

Bolsheviks Members of the Russian Social Democrat party, who followed Lenin and carried out a communist revolution in Russia in 1917

Boom Period of economic prosperity

'Buying on the margin' Borrowing money to buy shares on the stock market

Capitalism A system under which businesses are owned privately and people are able to make a profit

Communism A theory that society should be classless, private property abolished, and land and business owned collectively

Communists Followers of the ideas of Karl Marx, who believe in the theory of communism

Congress The US equivalent of parliament. Congress is split into two parts, the Senate and the House of Representatives

Consumer goods Manufactured goods that satisfy personal needs – vacuum cleaners, for example

Consumerism An increase in the production of consumer goods on the grounds that high spending is the basis of a sound economy

Credit Money available for borrowing

Depression A period of extended and severe decline in a nation's economy, marked by low production and high unemployment

Federal government The central government of the USA, based in Washington DC

Federal Reserve Board Organisation which controls the Federal Reserve – a national system of reserve cash available to banks

Flapper A young woman who flouted the norms of dress and behaviour in the 1920s

Fundamentalists Religious group who went to church frequently and believed in the Bible

General strike A strike by all or most of the workers in a country or province

Ghetto A city neighbourhood inhabited by a minority who live there because of social and economic pressure

Governor The elected head of a state within the USA

Gramophone A record player

Hobo An unemployed wanderer seeking a job

Hire purchase A system of credit whereby a person may purchase an item by making regular payments while having the use of it

Import duties Taxes placed on goods brought from foreign countries

Income tax A tax people have to pay on the money they earn

Industrialists Someone who owns and/or runs an industry or factory

Isolationism A policy of deliberately staying out of world affairs. The USA was isolationist between the two world wars

Jim Crow laws A series of laws which brought about segregation and discrimination against black Americans in the southern states of the USA

Laissez-faire A policy of no direct government interference in the economy

Lynching Put a person to death by hanging without a legal trial

Mass production Manufacture of goods on a large scale

Mechanisation The use of machines

Munitions Ammunition/weapons produced for the armed forces

National Association for the Advancement of Colored People (NAACP) Set up in 1909 to achieve better conditions for black Americans

'Open Door' policy Free admission of immigrants

Pogroms An organised violent attack against an ethnic group, usually Jews

Prohibition Banning of sale and consumption of alcohol

Rackets Schemes for obtaining money by illegal methods

Radicalism Wanting to bring about extreme social or political change

Red Scare Term used in the USA after the communist revolution in Russia in 1917. It was the fear that immigrants from Eastern Europe would bring ideas about a communist revolution to the USA

Republican Supporter of the Republican Party. Its main ideas were to keep taxes low, limit the powers of the federal government, follow policies which favoured business and encourage people to be self-sufficient

'Rugged individualism' The American ideal that individuals are responsible for their own lives without help from anyone else; they stand or fall by their own efforts

Socialist A belief in a society based on collective ownership of land and industry, and co-operation to benefit all

Glossary

Speakeasy An illegal drinking shop

Stock market The place where stocks and shares were bought and sold on a daily basis

Stocks and shares Certificates of ownership in a company

Supreme Court The highest federal court in the USA. It consists of nine judges, chosen by the president, who make sure that the president and Congress obey the rules of the Constitution

Tariff An import duty; a tax on foreign goods coming into a country

Temperance Movement An organisation which sought to outlaw the sale of alcoholic beverages

The 'Great Migration' Movement of farm workers in the USA in the 1930s

The Great Depression Slump in the economy in the 1930s which led to high unemployment

Trade union Organisations set up to protect and improve the rights of workers

Universal Negro Improvement Association (UNIA) A self-help organisation for black Americans set up in 1914 by Marcus Garvey

Wall Street Crash 29 October 1929, when more than 16 million shares were traded in panic selling, triggering further sales and leading to world economic crisis

Wall Street Base of New York's stock market

WASP White Anglo-Saxon Protestant

White supremacy The theory that white people are naturally superior to people of other races

Women's Movement A united effort to improve the social, economic and political position of women

Xenophobia An irrational fear or hatred of foreigners

Index

25 Point Programme 23, 28
Abyssinian invasion (Italy), effects 77
advertising, USA 132, 148, 154
African Americans *see* black Americans
agriculture (Germany) 17, 20, 28
airforce, Germany 75
alcohol, prohibition in USA 118–22
alliances with Germany 80, 87, 88
Americanisation of citizens 102, 110
anarchist activities, USA 105
Anglo-German Declaration 85
Anglo-German Naval Treaty 1935 77
Anschluss 74
Anti-Comitern Pact 80
Anti-Flirt Leagues 157
Anti-Saloon League 118, 119
anti-Semitism
    Nazi Party 60–5, 68, 71
    USA 105, 114
appeasement policy 83, 86
armistice, Germany's viewpoint 8
Armstrong, Louis 147
army (Germany)
    allegiance to Hitler 45, 46
    conscription and increase size 48, 77
    in Munich *Pusch* 25–6
    Reichswehr 10, 11, 12
army (USA), women in 152
art
    censorship in Third Reich 73
    Weimar Republic 21
Article 48 6, 22, 30
Aryan race 24, 60, 67
assembly lines, in mass production 130
Austria, *Anschluss* 76, 81–3
Bamberg Conference 28
beer production ban 119
Bible Belt 108–9, 146, 149
black Americans
    jazz musicians 146–7, 150
    oppression 105, 111, 113, 115–17
Black Thursday 138
Black Tuesday 138, 139
books, censorship in Third Reich 72
bootlegging 123
Bow, Clara 144, 145, 155
brewing industry, USA 121
Britain
    declares war on Germany 89
    guarantee to Poland 87
    and Hitler 75, 77, 78, 84–5
    post WW1 agreements 17, 18
    relations with Italy and France 18, 75, 77, 79, 80, 84–5, 87
Brooks, Louise 155
Brownshirts (SA) 24, 35, 44–5, 68
Brüning, Heinrich 30, 33
Butler Act (Tennessee, USA) 109

Capone, Al 123
car industry, USA 130–1
Catholic Church
    in Nazi Germany 58
    persecution in USA 105, 112, 114
censorship 32, 42, 72, 73
centralisation of Germany 43
Centre Party (Germany) 30, 33, 38, 42, 43
Chamberlain, Neville 83, 84
Chaplin, Charlie 144, 145
childbearing, in Third Reich 51, 52, 53, 54
cinema
    Nazi Germany 21, 71
    USA 142–5
communism
Anti-Comitern pact 80
fear in US 104–5, 107, 112
Hitler's hatred of 74
suppression in Germany 11, 12, 41, 42
see also Communist Party; Soviet Union
Communist Party (KPD) (Germany)
    election results 19, 31, 33, 38, 42
    growth 29, 31
    Red Front Fighters 35
    suppression 41, 42, 43
    uprisings 11, 12
compulsory labour service 47
concentration camps 43, 68–9
concordat, with Pope Pius XI 58
conscription, Germany 48, 77
Constitution (Weimar) 6–7
consumerism (USA) 129, 132, 136
    among women 154
Coolidge, Calvin (US President) 134
corruption, USA 122, 123, 125–6
Crawford, Joan 155
credit policies, impact of 137
crime (Germany)
    arrests for 'political crimes' 67
    massacres 44–5
crime (USA)
    during prohibition 120, 122
    Ku Klux Klan attacks 113, 114
    organised crime 123–4
culture
    Germany 21, 71, 72, 73
    USA 142–50
curriculum, Third Reich 55, 62
Czechoslovakia, invasion 84–6
Dachau concentration camp 43
dance marathons 149
dancing, USA 149, 156
Danzig 87
Daugherty, Harry 125, 126
Dawes Plan 15–16
Decree for the Protection of People and State 41
department stores, USA 133

Deutsche Arbeitsfront (DAF) 43, 49, 50
dictatorship in Germany 42
Disarmament Conference 75
Dolchstoss theory 8
Dollfuss, Engelbert, assassination 76
Du Bois, W.E.B. 116
Ebert, Friedrich 6, 11, 43
economy
    Germany 13–17, 29–30, 33, 47–8
    USA 127–34, 135–41
education in Third Reich 55–7, 62
elections (Germany) 19, 33, 38, 40, 43
electrificaton, benefits in America 129
Ellington, Duke 147
Emergency Quota Act (USA) 102
employment
    black Americans 115
    Germany 43, 47–8, 49–51, 77
    women 20, 51, 53, 151, 152
Enabling Act 42, 43
entertainment *see* culture
evolution, fundamentalist view 108–9
extremism *see* political extremism
Fall, Albert 125, 126
fashion, US flappers 156
feminist movement, USA 154–5
films *see* cinema
financial crises
    hyperinflation in Germany 13–17
    losses in Wall Street Crash 140, 141
First World War
    effect on America 102, 128, 152
    effect on Germany 6–14, 128
'flappers' 146, 148, 154–7
forced labour, concentration camps 68
Ford, Henry 130–1
Fordney-McCumber Tariff 134
foreign policy (Germany)
    in 25 Point Programme 23
    Alliances 80, 87, 88
    Anschluss 76, 81–3
    Czechoslovakia 84–6
    Hitler as Chancellor1933–5 75–7
    League of Nations 18, 75
    Poland 75, 87, 88, 89
    rearmament 48, 75, 77
    Rhineland 1936 78–9
    Weimar Republic 18
France
    declares war on Germany 89
    occupation of Ruhr 13
    relations with Britain and Italy 18, 75, 77, 79, 80
Free Polish Forces 89
Freikorps 11, 12, 92
fundamentalism 108–9, 146, 149
gangsters in USA 120, 123–4
Garbo, Greta 144

172

Index

Garvey, Marcus 117
Geheime Staatspolizei (Gestapo) 66, 67, 68
general elections, Germany 19, 33, 38, 40, 43
'German Christians' 59
German cinema 21, 71
German Faith Movement 58
German Labour Front (DAF) 43, 49, 50
German Lawyers Front 70
Gestapo 66, 67, 68
ghettos
    Germany 65
    USA 102
Gleichschaltung 43, 70
Goebbels, Josef
    behind Kristallnacht 64
    propaganda 28, 32, 34, 35, 40, 71–2
    on role of women 51
Goering, Hermann 40, 44, 67
gramophone industry 148
Great Depression 29–30, 135–6, 140–1
'Great Migration, The' 115
Harding, Warren (US President) 125
Hays Code 145
Heydrich, Reinhard 67
Himmler, Heinrich 26, 66, 67
Hindenburg, Paul von
    attitude to Hitler 38, 39, 40, 41
    election as president 19, 34
    life 39, 46
hire purchase 133, 137
Hitler, Adolf
    25 Point Programme 23
    aggression towards Poland 87
    appeal and charisma 36–7
    art opinions 73
    becomes Chancellor 22, 30, 38–9
    Enabling Act 42–3
    expansion of Germany 81, 84–6, 88
    foreign policy 74–89
    Führer title 23, 46
    hatred of communism 74
    legal system control 70
    Mein Kampf 27, 32, 55, 61, 74
    at Munich Conference 84–5, 86
    and Mussolini 25, 76, 77, 80, 85, 87
    powerful speaker 22, 23, 24, 37
    becomes President 46
    presidential election 1932 34
    seizes power 40–6
    Soviet Union fears 77, 84
    support from industrialists 35, 40
    and Treaty of Versailles 74, 75
    trial and imprisonment 27
    unemployment schemes 47–8
    and Weimar Government 16, 24, 25, 27, 33
Hitler Youth (*HitlerJugend*) 28, 56, 57
Hollywood 145
Hossbach Memorandum 81
housing (Germany), construction 19
hyperinflation, Germany 13–17
immigrants to USA
    as cheap labour force 127
    opposition to 101–3, 105, 107, 113, 114

Immigration Act (USA) 102
import tariffs 134, 136
Indian Citizenship Act 110
individualism in USA 134
industry
    Germany 16, 17, 20, 35, 40
    USA 129–31
inflation, Germany 13–17
intelligence services, Third Reich 67
invisible unemployment 48
isolationism, USA 102, 134
Italy
    Abyssinian invasion 77
    relations with Britain and France 18, 75, 77, 79, 80
Japan, Anti-Comitern Pact 80
jazz 146–7, 154–5
Jazz Singer (film) 145
Jews
    Hitler's denouncement 24, 27, 28, 33
    persecution in Germany 48, 60–5
    persecution in USA 105, 114
Jim Crow laws 111
job creation schemes, Germany 47–8, 77
judges, authority in Third Reich 70
Kapp *Putsch* 12
Keaton, Joseph 'Buster' 144, 145
Kellogg-Briand Pact 18
KPD *see* Communist Party (KPD) (Germany)
Kraft durch Freude (KdF) 50
Kristallnacht 64
Ku Klux Klan 112–14
Labour Front 43, 49, 50
laissez-faire policy, USA 134, 137
Länder, Reich government 43
Law Against the Formation of Parties 43
Law for the Encouragement of Marriage 52
Law for the Protection of German Blood and Honour 63
League of German Maidens 52, 56, 57
League of Nations 8, 18, 75, 76, 77
Lebensborn programme 52
Lebensraum 74, 84
legal system, Nazi control 70
legislation
    Germany 42, 43, 52, 63
    USA 102, 103, 109, 119
literature in Germany 21, 72
Locarno Pact 18, 78
luxury goods, in USA 129, 132
lynchings, USA 111, 113, 116
McPherson, Aimee Semple 108
marriage, in Third Reich 52, 54, 60, 63
marriage loans 52, 53
mass production, in America 130–1
massacres, purges by Hitler and SS 44–5
media
    in Nazi Germany 32, 34, 40, 41, 71–2, 73
    portrayal of US strikes 104
Mein Kampf 27, 32, 55, 61, 74
Meriam Report on Native Americans 110

Monkey Trial 109
morality
    Germany 51–8
    USA 108, 118–19, 145, 146, 149
Mother's Cross 52
movie stars, USA 144, 145, 155
movies, popularity 142–5
    see also cinema
Müller, Ludwig 59
Munich Conference 84–5, 86
Munich *Putsch* 25–6
music
    censorship in Third Reich 73
    popular music in USA 146–7, 148, 154–5
Mussolini, Bernito 25, 76, 77, 80, 85
National Association for the Advancement of Colored People (NAACP) 116
National Labour Service Corps 47
National Origins Act (USA) 102, 103
National Party (DNVP) 19, 33, 35, 38–9, 42
National Socialist League for the Maintenance of Law 70
Native Americans, oppression 110
Nazi Party (NSDAP)
    ban 26, 28
    coalition with National Party 38–9
    consolidation of power 40–6
    in elections 19, 30, 33, 38, 42, 43
    funding 35, 40
    Munich *Putsch* 25–6
    political manifesto 23
    propaganda 28, 32, 34, 35, 40, 60, 71–2
    rise 22–3, 24, 28, 32–4, 35–7
    SD intelligence service 67
    see also Hitler, Adolf; Third Reich
Nazi-Soviet Pact 88
Nazi Teachers' League 55
newspapers
    censorship 32, 41, 73
    as political tool 32, 34, 104
Night of the Long Knives 44–5
November Criminals 8, 33
Nuremberg Laws 63
Ohio Gang 125
Open Door policy (USA) 101
Operation Hummingbird 44–5
organised crime 123–4
over-production in USA 135
over-speculation in USA 137
Pact of Steel 87
Palmer Raids 105
panic selling, Wall Street Crash 138
Pastors' Emergency League 59
peace initiatives in Europe 18
    see also Treaty of Versailles
People's Courts, Third Reich 70
persecution
    in Germany 48, 60–5
    in USA 105, 112–13, 114
Pickford, Mary 144, 145
plays, censorship in Third Reich 73
Poland, invasion 75, 87, 88–9
Polish Corridor 87

173

political extremism
    in Germany 28–37, 38-9, 40-6
    in USA 112–14
political prisoners, Third Reich 68
popular music in USA 146-7, 148, 154-5
posters, for propaganda 72
presidents (Germany)
    elections 31, 34
    Ebert, Friedrich 6, 11, 43
    Hindenburg, Paul von 19, 34, 38, 39, 40, 41, 46
    Hitler assumes role 46
presidents (USA) 119, 125, 134
prisoners in concentration camps 68
prohibition 118–22, 123
Prohibition Amendment 119
propaganda in Germany
    in school curriculum 55, 62
    use by Nazis 28, 32, 34, 35, 40, 60, 71-2
protectionism in USA 134
Protestant Church, in Nazi Germany 59
race riots, USA 115
racial policy, Third Reich 48, 52, 60–5
racism
    persecution of Jews 48, 60-5, 105, 114
    in USA 102, 104, 106-7, 112, 113
radio
    Nazi use for propaganda 32, 34, 71
    spread in USA 148
rallies, Nazi 34, 36
rearmament
    Britain 86
    Germany 48, 77
Red Front Fighters 35
'Red Scare 104, 107
Reich Law on Citizenship 63
Reich Office for Jewish Emigration 65
Reichsarbeitsdienst (RAD) 47
Reichsmark 16
Reichstag 6, 19
Reichstag fire 40–1
Reichswehr (army) 10, 11, 12
religion
    opposed by Nazis 58–9, 68
    in USA 102, 108-9, 112, 146, 149
    see also Jews
Rentenmark 16
reparation payments 8, 9, 13, 15–16, 30
Rhineland, German re-occupation 78–9
Ribbentrop-Molotov Pact 88
Röhm, Ernst 35, 44, 45
Rome-Berlin Alliance 80
Ruhr, occupation by France 13, 15
Russia 77, 84, 85, 88
SA (*Sturmateilung*) 24, 35, 44-5, 68
Saarland, returned to Germany 76
Sacco, Nicola, trial 106-7
St Valentine's Day Massacre 124
'Scarface' 123
Schuschnigg, Kurt (Austrian Chancellor) 81

Schutzaffel (SS) 28, 44, 45, 60, 66, 67, 68
Scott Fitzgerald, F. (novelist) 150, 155
SD (*Sicherheitsdienst*) 66, 67
Second World War, outbreak 88–9
segregation
    black people in America 111
    Jews in Germany 65
shares, stock market 137, 138
silent movies 143
smuggling, during prohibition 120
Social Democrat Party (SPD) 19, 30, 33, 38, 42, 43
social policies, Third Reich 51–8
'Soviet Ark' 105
Soviet Union 77, 84, 85, 88
Spartacist Uprising 11
speakeasies 120, 121, 150, 156
speculation, U.S. stock exchange 137
SS 28, 44, 45, 60, 66, 67, 68
Stalin, Joseph
    considers alliance with Britain 87
    Nazi-Soviet Pact 88
    not invited to Munich conference 85
standard of living, Germany 19
state control, Germany 43, 49–59
state police, Third Reich 66, 67, 68
Stephenson, David 113
stock market problems, USA 137–40
Strasser, Gregor 28, 45
Strength through Joy 50
Stresa Front 77
Stresemann, G. 14, 15, 16, 18, 19, 29
strikes, Germany 12, 13, 16
Sturmabteilung (SA) 24, 35, 44-5, 68
Sudetenland Crisis 84-5
suffrage, USA 153
supermarkets 133
Swanson, Gloria 142, 144, 145
swastika 24, 70
'talkies' (films) 145
tariffs on trade 134, 136
Teapot Dome scandal 126
technology, USA 128–30
Temperance Movement 118
terror tactics 66–9, 113, 114
Thälmann, Ernst 31
Thayer, Judge Webster 107
theatre, censorship in Third Reich 73
Third Reich
    anti-Semitism 60–5
    censorship of the arts 71, 72, 73
    economic policies 47–50
    education policies 55–7, 62
    foundation 42
    racial policies 52, 60–5
    religious policies 58–60
    removal of opposition 43–6
    social policies 51–8
    territory expansion 74
    women's role 51–3
    see also Nazi Party (NSDAP)

trade unions
    Germany 12, 35, 42, 43, 49, 50
    USA 105
Treaty of Versailles
    breaking of terms 77
    German resentment of 8–9, 33
    Hitler's reversal aims 74, 75
    Locarno Pact changes 18
unemployment
    Germany 16, 19, 22, 29, 47–8
    USA 135, 140
unemployment insurance 19
Universal Negro Improvement Association (UNIA) 117
uprisings, Weimar Republic 10–12
Valentino, Rudolph 144, 145
Vanzetti, Bartolomeo, trial 106-7
Versailles Peace Treaty *see* Treaty of Versailles
Volkswagen scheme 49
Volstead Act 119
von Papen, Franz 38, 39, 40
von Schleicher, Kurt 38, 45
wage increases, Germany 19, 49
Wall Street Crash 28, 29, 33, 135–41
Walsh, Thomas 126
War Guilt Clause 8
WASP citizen profile 102
Wehrmacht see army
Weimar Government
    attacks by Hitler 24, 25, 27, 33
    Constitutions 6–7
    impact of Great Depression 30
    inflation 13, 14–15
    loans from USA 16, 17
    political instability 10–12
    political power 19, 30
    support 10, 12
    Treaty of Versailles 8
Weimar Republic 6–21, 30, 42
    see also Weimar Government
welfare benefits, Germany 19
white supremacy 112–14
Wilson, Woodrow (US President) 119
women (Germany)
    employment 20, 51, 53, 54
    oppression in Third Reich 51–3
    in Weimer Republic 20, 51
women (USA)
    changing role 151-2, 153
    influence of jazz 154–7
    and prohibition 118, 119, 121
work books 43, 49
working conditions
    for black Americans 115
    in Third Reich 43, 47, 49, 50
    in Weimer Republic 16, 19
xenophobia in America 104, 106-7
    see also Jews, persecution
Young Plan 16

Acknowledgements

The Publishers would like to thank the following for permission to reproduce copyright material.

p.5 © The Print Collector/Alamy Stock Photo; **p.9** © Gary Lucken/fotoLibra; **p.11** © Stapleton Historical Collection/HIP/TopFoto; **p.12** © ullstein bild via Getty Images; **p.14** (left) © World History Archive/TopFoto; (right) © ullstein bild/TopFoto; **p.15** © IMAGNO/Austrian Archives/TopFoto; **p.18** © Imagno/Getty Images; **p.20** © SZ Photo/Scherl/Bridgeman Images; **p.21** © Estate of George Grosz, Princeton, N.J. /DACS 2017/Nationalegalerie, SMB/Jörg P. Anders/bpk; **p.25** © Heinrich Hoffmann/ullstein bild/Getty Images; **p.26** © akg-images; **p.27** © Hulton-Deutsch Collection/CORBIS/Corbis via Getty Images; **p.29** © Walter Ballhause/akg-images; **p.31** © akg-images; **p.32** (left) © Randall Bytwerk, German Propaganda Archive; (right) © Ullstein Bild/akg-images; **p.34** © Randall Bytwerk, German Propaganda Archive; **p.35** (top) © The Heartfield Community of Heirs/VG Bild-Kunst, Bonn and DACS, London 2017/akg-images; (bottom) © SZ Photo/Scherl/Bridgeman Images; **p.36** © Hulton Archive/Getty Images; **p.37** © The Print Collector/Print Collector/Getty Images; **p.39** (top left) © Pictorial Press Ltd/Alamy Stock Photo; (top right) © Chronicle/Alamy Stock Photo; (bottom) © Punch Limited; **p.40** © Topham Picturepoint; **p.41** (left) © Bettmann/Getty Images; (right) © Bettmann/Getty Images; **p.43** © R. Paul Evans; **p.44** © Bettmann/Getty Images; **p.45** © Evening Standard/Solo Syndication (photo: British Cartoon Archive, University of Kent); **p.46** © Hulton Archive/Getty Images; **p.47** © ullsteinbild/TopFoto; **p.48** © Institut für Stadtgeschichte Frankfurt am Main; **p.49** © Hulton-Deutsch Collection/CORBIS/Corbis via Getty Images; **p.50** © akg-images; **p.51** © akg-images; **p.52** (left) By courtesy of the Wiener Library; **p.56** (left) © akg-images; (right) © ullsteinbild/TopFoto; **p.57** © akg-images; **pg. 59** (left) ©akg-images; (right) © The Heartfield Community of Heirs/VG Bild-Kunst, Bonn and DACS, London 2017, Photo Mary Evans Picture Library; **p.60** © akg-images; **p.61** © Mary Evans/Weimar Archive; **p.62** © 1999 Topham Picturepoint/TopFoto; **p.65** © World History Archive/TopFoto; **p.66** (top) © Bettmann/Getty Images; (bottom) © ullsteinbild/TopFoto; **p.69** © akg-images/ullstein bild; **p.70** © bpk; **p.71** © SZ Photo/Scherl/Bridgeman Images; **p.72** (left) © TopFoto; (right) © Ullstein Bild/akg-images; **p.73** © Mary Evans/Weimar Archive; **p.76** © Hulton-Deutsch Collection/CORBIS/Corbis via Getty Images; **p.77** © World History Archive/Alamy Stock Photo; **p.78** © Hulton-Deutsch Collection/CORBIS/Corbis via Getty Images; **p.79** © Punch Limited; **p.80** © INTERFOTO/Alamy Stock Photo; **p.82** © ullstein bild/ullstein bild via Getty Images; **p.85** © dpa picture alliance/Alamy Stock Photo; **p.88** (left) © Solo Syndication/Associated Newspapers Ltd (British Cartoon Archive, University of Kent); (right) © Solo Syndication/Associated Newspapers Ltd (British Cartoon Archive, University of Kent); **p.91** © Ullsteinbild/TopFoto; **p.92** © Stapleton Historical Collection/HIP/TopFoto; **p.94** © Jackie Fox/fotoLibra; **p.95** © Solo Syndication/Associated Newspapers Ltd (British Cartoon Archive, University of Kent); **p.100** © The Bain Collection via Library of Congress/LC-DIG-ggbain-30546; **p.103** © Private Collection/ Peter Newark American Pictures / The Bridgeman Art Library; **p.104** © Library and Archives, Historical Society of Western Pennsylvania; **p.105** © Joseph A. Labadie Collection, University of Michigan Library (Special Collections Library)/Palmer Raid(s) LPF.0853; **p.106** © Bettmann/Getty Images; **p.107** © Bettmann/Getty Images; **p.109** © The Granger Collection, NYC/TopFoto; **p.110** © Bettmann/Getty Images; **p.111** (left) © Bettmann/Getty Images; (right) © The Granger Collection, NYC/TopFoto; **p.112** © Library of Congress, Prints and Photographs Division; **p.116** © Granamour Weems Collection/Alamy Stock Photo; **p.117** © Everett Collection Historical/Alamy Stock Photo; **p.118** © The Granger Collection/TopFoto; **p.119** (top) © Ohio State University; (bottom) © Minnesota Historical Society, K4.2 p10. Negative number 22082; **p.120** © Library of Congress, Prints and Photographs Division, LC-USZ62-100533; **p.121** © Photo Researchers, Inc/Alamy Stock Photo; **p.122** (top) © Private Collection/ Peter Newark American Pictures / The Bridgeman Art Library; (bottom) © IMAGNO/Austrian Archives/Getty Images; **p.123** (top) Public domain/https://commons.wikimedia.org/wiki/File:Al_Capone_in_1930.jpg; (bottom) © Library of Congress/Corbis/VCG via Getty Images; **p.124** © Private Collection/ Peter Newark American Pictures/ The Bridgeman Art Library; **p.125** © Granger Historical Picture Archive/Alamy Stock Photo; **p.126** © MPI/Getty Images; **p.127** © Private Collection/Peter Newark American Pictures / The Bridgeman Art Library; **p.128** © akg-images/Alamy Stock Photo; **p.129** © Everett Collection Historical/Alamy Stock Photo; **p.131** © ullsteinbild/TopFoto; **p.132** © Mary Evans Picture Library; **p.133** © Poland, Clifford H./Library of Congress/Corbis/VCG via Getty Images; p.136 © The Granger Collection, NYC/TopFoto; **p.139** © Bettmann/Getty Images; **p.140** © Ullsteinbild/ Topfoto; **p.141** © Charles Deering McCormick Library of Special Collections, Northwestern University Libraries; **p.143** © Hulton-Deutsch Collection/CORBIS/Corbis via Getty Images; **p.144** © (top left) Library of Congress Prints and Photographs Division Washington, D.C./LC-B2- 5470-19; (top right) Library of Congress Prints and Photographs Division Washington, D.C/LC-B2- 5106-15; (bottom left) © Pictorial Press Ltd/Alamy Stock Photo; (bottom right) © AF archive/Alamy Stock Photo; **p.145** © Bettmann/Getty Images; **p.147** (top) © Bettmann/Getty Images; (middle) © William Gottlieb/Redferns/Getty Images; (bottom) © JP Jazz Archive/Redferns/Getty Images; **p.148** © Everett Collection Historical/Alamy Stock Photo; **p.149** (top) © Bettmann/Getty Images; (bottom) © The Granger Collection, NYC/TopFoto; **p.150** © Granger Historical Picture Archive/Alamy Stock Photo; **p.151** © Bettmann/Getty Images; **p.152** © Shutterstock/Everett Historical; **p.153** © Granger Historical Picture Archive/Alamy Stock Photo; **p.154** © Glasshouse Images/Alamy Stock Photo; **p.157** © Bettmann/Getty Images; **p.159** © Bettmann/Getty Images; **p.160** © Ullsteinbild/ Topfoto; **p.162** © Bettmann/Getty Images; **p.163** © MPI/Getty Images

p.69 Edward Adler testimony, Holocaust Encyclopedia, U.S. Holocaust Memorial Museum.

Every effort has been made to trace all copyright holders, but if any have been inadvertently overlooked, the Publishers will be pleased to make the necessary arrangements at the first opportunity.